THE WIZARD OF THE SEA

or, A Trip Under the Ocean

ROY ROCKWOOD

1st WORLD
LIBRARY
Literary Society

The Wizard of the Sea

Roy Rockwood

© 1st World Library, 2008
PO Box 2211
Fairfield, IA 52556
www.1stworldlibrary.com
First Edition

LCCN: 2007935410

Softcover ISBN: 978-1-4218-9361-7
Hardcover ISBN: 978-1-4218-9461-4
eBook ISBN: 978-1-4218-9261-0

Purchase *"The Wizard of the Sea"*
as a traditional bound book at:
www.1stWorldLibrary.com/purchase.asp?ISBN=978-1-4218-9361-7

1st World Library is a literary, educational organization
dedicated to:

- Creating a free internet library of downloadable ebooks

- Hosting writing competitions and offering book publishing
scholarships.

**Interested in more 1st World Library books? contact:
literacy@1stworldlibrary.com
Check us out at: www.1stworldlibrary.com**

1ˢᵗ World Library Literary Society

Giving Back to the World

"If you want to work on the core problem, it's early school literacy."

- James Barksdale, former CEO of Netscape

"No skill is more crucial to the future of a child, or to a democratic and prosperous society, than literacy."

- Los Angeles Times

"Literacy... means far more than learning how to read and write... The aim is to transmit... knowledge and promote social participation."

- UNESCO

"Literacy is not a luxury, it is a right and a responsibility. If our world is to meet the challenges of the twenty-first century we must harness the energy and creativity of all our citizens."

- President Bill Clinton

"Parents should be encouraged to read to their children, and teachers should be equipped with all available techniques for teaching literacy, so the varying needs and capacities of individual kids can be taken into account."

- Hugh Mackay

CONTENTS

CHAPTER I

INTRODUCING OUR HEROES

"Hip, hurrah! Hip, hurrah!"

"Well, I declare; Mont Folsom, what is the matter with you?"

"Matter? Nothing is the matter, Tom, only I'm going to a boarding school—just the best place on the face of the earth, too—Nautical Hall, on the seacoast."

"Humph! I didn't know as how a boarding school was such a jolly place," grumbled old Tom Barnstable. "They'll cane ye well if ye git into mischief, lad."

"Will they, Tom? What for? I never do any wrong," and Mont Folsom put on a very sober face.

"Jest to hear the lad! Never do no mischief! Ha! ha! Why you're the wust boy in the town fer mischief, Mont—an' everybody knows it. A nautical school, did ye say. Maybe they'll take ye out in a ship some time in that case."

"They do take the pupils out—every summer, so Carl Barnaby was telling me. He goes there, you know, and so does Link Harmer."

"Then you an' Carl will make a team—an' Heaven help the folks as comes in your way," added Tom Barnstable decidedly.

"But we are not so bad, I tell you, Tom," said Mont, but with a sly twinkle in his bright eyes.

"Oh, no, not at all. But jest you tell me who drove the cow into Squire Borden's dining room and who stuffed the musical instruments of the brass band with sawdust at the Fourth of July celebration? You never do anything, you little innocent lamb!"

And with a loud guffaw the old character sauntered down the street toward his favorite resort, the general store.

Montrose Folsom continued on his way. He was a handsome youth of fifteen, tall and square-shouldered, with a taking way about him that had made him a host of friends. He was the only son of Mrs. Alice Folsom, a rich widow.

A moment after leaving Tom Barnstable, Mont reached the home of his particular chum, Lincoln Harmer. Throwing open the gate, he espied Link in the barnyard, and made a rush forward.

"Hurrah! hurrah! hurrah!"

"That settles it, Mont, you're going with me next term!" exclaimed Link, a bright fellow of our hero's age.

"If I wasn't I'd sing a dirge instead of shouting, Link. Yes, it's all settled, and I'll be ready to start with you Monday."

"Your mother has written to Captain Hooper?"

Roy Rockwood

"Yes, and got word back in to-day's mail."

"Good!"

"I'm to buy a lot of things down to Carley's store and then go home and start to pack up. Come on."

Arm in arm, the two chums made their way to the large general store, where Tom Barnstable was again encountered. Here Mont purchased some extra underclothing his mother said he needed. While he was at this Tom Barnstable came close to him.

"When are ye goin' away?" he asked.

"Monday morning, six o'clock."

"Don't fergit the old man, Mont. We've had lots of good times—fishin' an' huntin', ye know."

That was Tom Barnstable, good-natured and willing to do, but an absolute beggar at the slightest chance.

"I won't forget you, Tom, not I," said the merry-hearted lad. "Here you are," and he slipped a shining dollar into the man's hand. A moment later he called one of the store clerks aside.

"Have you any of those April-fool cigars left?" he whispered.

"Yes—just four."

"I'll take them."

The cigars bought and paid for, the boy put three of them in an inside pocket and then turned the fourth over to Tom Barnstable.

"Here, Tom, put the pipe away and have a real Havana to celebrate the parting," he said, and the old man immediately did as requested.

The cigar burnt all right for just half a minute. Then something began to bulge at the end. It kept growing larger and larger, forming into what is called a Pharaoh's serpent, three or four feet long.

Tom Barnstable's eyes began to blaze. He stared at Mont wildly.

"Who—what—what is that?" he stammered. "Great Scott! I've got 'em!"

And, dashing the weed to the floor, he rushed from the country store, with the boys' laugh ringing in his ears.

"He'll remember you now, no doubt of that!" said Link merrily.

The day was Saturday, and it was a busy one for both Mont and Link, with packing trunks and bags, and getting ready otherwise.

The Sabbath passed quietly enough, and five o'clock Monday morning found the two boys on their way to Nautical Hall.

The run of the train was to New York, and here they fell in with their mutual chum, Carl Barnaby, a rich young fellow from their town, and several others who will be introduced as our story progresses.

From the Metropolis the boys took another train directly for the seacoast. At Pemberton they had to change cars, and here they met several more scholars of Nautical Hall.

"There is Ike Brosnan and Hoke Ummer!" cried Link. "Two of our fellows."

The newcomers were quickly introduced. Ike Brosnan looked a whole-souled fellow and full of fun. Hoke Ummer, on the other hand, seemed of a decidedly sour turn of mind.

"Hoke is a good deal of a bully," whispered Link, later on. "You want to steer clear of him."

"Thanks; he'll not step on my toes," returned Mont firmly. "The first man who tries to haze or bully me will get his fingers burnt."

"Oh, the boys will be sure to want a little fun. You mustn't be too particular."

"I don't mean that—I mean they mustn't go too far," replied Mont.

Little did he dream of all the hazings and larks to be played ere that school term should be over.

The journey to the seacoast was devoid of any special incident. The ride on the train was magnificent, and all enjoyed it thoroughly.

Towards nightfall a landing was made not many miles from Eagle Point. Here at the dock a long stage was in waiting to take them to the Hall. The four boys, along with a dozen others, got aboard, and they moved off rapidly for Nautical Hall, two miles distant.

CHAPTER II

A TERRIFIC EXPLOSION

Nautical Hall was a large building of brick, stone, and wood situated at the top of a small hill. In front was a level parade ground, and to one side the grounds sloped down to the edge of a small bay, while at the other they were flanked by a heavy wood.

The institution was owned and managed by Captain Hooper, an ex-army and -navy officer, who looked to the military drill of the boys and left the educational department to an able corps of assistants. With the assistants and the gallant captain himself we will become better acquainted as our tale proceeds.

Mont soon became acquainted with nearly all of the one hundred and odd boys who attended Nautical Hall, and became the leader of a set composed of himself, Link Harmer, Barry Powell, another lively lad, Carl Barnaby, his old-time chum, Piggy Mumps, a fat youth, and Sam Schump, a German pupil, as good-natured as can possibly be imagined.

As soon as the boys arrived they were assigned to their places. Mont was put in the room with the crowd above

Roy Rockwood

mentioned. This room connected with another, in which were installed the bully, Hoke Ummer; Bill Goul, his toady, and half a dozen of the bully's cronies.

"This room will get into a free fight with that gang some day," was Barry Powell's comment, after Schump, the German boy, had related how the bully had treated him.

"Dot's it, mine gracious," replied Sam Schump. "Ve vill git togedder an' show dem vot ve can do, aint it!"

Several days were spent in getting ready for the term. Mont was placed in the first class, with twenty others, and he was likewise put in an awkward squad to learn the steps and manual of arms, for the boys had regular military and naval exercises.

As luck would have it, our hero was placed under one of the assistant teachers, and fared very well, but poor Piggy Mumps was put in a squad under Hoke Ummer, who did all he could to make the fat boy miserable.

"Eyes right! Eyes left! Front!" shouted Hoke. "Why don't you mind, you clown!" he added to poor Piggy, who was in a sweat to do as ordered.

"Vot you say, eyes right an' den eyes left, ven da vos right?" asked Piggy innocently.

"Silence! Eyes right! Eyes left! You clown, can't you twist your eyes, or are you too fat?" roared Hoke.

"Ton't vos call me a clown, you—you unchentlemanly poy!" cried Piggy wrathfully, when without warning Hoke fell upon him and hit him a blow on the neck.

This was too much for Piggy, and he ran out of the line and closed with the bully. But he was no match for the big boy, and Piggy would have been severely punished had not Hoke been caught by the shoulder and hurled backward against a wall.

"Let him alone!" came in the voice of Mont. "You have no right to touch him, Hoke Ummer."

"Haven't I, though?" sneered the bully. "Do you suppose I'm going to be made a fool of by a lump of fat like that? You clear out, or I'll give you a dose, too!"

"You can try it on any time you please," replied our hero quietly.

"A fight! A fight!" exclaimed half a dozen at once, and the awkward squad was broken up on the instant.

"A fight?" repeated the bully. "He'll get a thrashing—that's all it will amount to. Come on down to the woods if you want to have it out."

"I'm willing to meet you," returned Mont, and started along, followed by Piggy, Link, and a dozen others.

But scarcely had the boys gone a rod before the belfry bell rang out loudly five times.

That was the signal for assembly on the parade grounds.

"Hullo, we can't go now!" cried Link. "Boys, you'll have to postpone that mill till later."

"I'll meet you after assembly," growled Hoke Ummer, under his breath, as Captain Hooper put in an appearance.

"I'll be ready any time," rejoined our hero.

"Boys, we are to have visitors in fifteen minutes!" shouted out Captain Hooper. "Attention! The captains will form their companies on the campus and a salute will be fired as the visitors enter the grounds."

Orders were quickly passed, and inside of five minutes the boy cadets were drawn up in long lines, with the officers of the two companies in their proper places.

The visitors were old friends of the captain who had come to the Hall merely out of curiosity. As their carriages approached, a cannon was run out, and Link and several others were detailed to fire it off.

Link chose Mont to assist, and before long all was in readiness to touch her off.

"Here they come!" shouted somebody.

"Stand ready to fire!" sang out Captain Hooper, in true military style. "Steady, boys, now—I expect all to make the best possible appearance. Fire!"

Link touched the cannon off, while our hero and several others stood close at hand.

Bang!

The report was terrific. The old cannon was overcharged, and was blown into a thousand pieces, which flew in all directions.

Both Link and Mont were hurled flat, and while the former was seen to stagger up again, our hero lay as one dead!

CHAPTER III

THE GREAT FIGHT

"He is dead!"

"Run for the doctor!"

"A piece struck me, too!"

"The cannon must have been overloaded!"

Such were some of the cries which went up after the awful explosion.

Captain Hooper stood close at hand, and instantly went to our hero's assistance.

He caught the youth up in his arms and carried him to a shady spot.

"Bring some water," he commanded, but water was already at hand. With it he bathed Mont's head.

For a minute there was an intense silence. Then, with a quiver, the lad opened his eyes.

"Wha—what—Did the cannon burst?" he asked feebly.

"Hurrah! He's all right!" shouted Link joyfully, and inside of five minutes more Mont stood up and gazed about him in wonder.

But he was too weak to take part in the review, and while this went on sat in a rustic chair under the oak tree, with several of the lady visitors by his side.

The reception to the guests over, the cadets were dismissed, and the crowd lost no time in dispersing.

Link remained with his chum, and both walked towards the lake.

"How do you feel?" asked Link anxiously.

"Rather faint in the legs, to tell the truth," was the reply. "But I guess I'll soon get over it."

"Ready to do that fighting?" demanded a rough voice at their elbow, and Hoke Ummer ranged up at their side.

"For shame, Hoke, Mont isn't in condition, and you know it," said Link.

"Oh, nonsense!" growled the bully. "That cannon affair was only a fake. He wasn't hurt a bit."

This remark angered our hero, and, stepping up, he faced the bully defiantly.

"I will fight you whenever you say," he said stoutly.

A boy standing near heard the remark, and the news spread

like magic.

"A fight between Hoke and Mont. Come on down to the woods."

The schoolboy cadets needed no second invitation. A score started from the campus instantly.

They were about evenly divided as to who would win.

The bully was known to be heavy and strong.

Yet our hero had shown lots of pluck.

In a corner of the grounds, shut out from view from the school windows by a belt of trees, the boys assembled to witness the conflict.

Mont prepared for the encounter, assisted by Link.

Ummer, satisfied of an easy victory, placed himself in the hands of his toady and backer, Bill Goul.

When the combatants were declared ready they faced each other.

As Hoke looked into the unflinching eyes of his opponent the smile of satisfaction he had worn for the past few hours suddenly faded.

He could see he must do his best to win.

"But I'll mash him, see if I don't," he said to his toadies.

"That's right, Hoke!"

"Show him what you can do."

Mont said nothing.

"He's a tough one," whispered Link. "Beware of a foul."

"I'll have my eyes open."

The boys took off their coats and vests.

A ring was formed and our hero and the bully got into position.

"Time!" cried one of the older boys, and the great fight began.

At first Mont was cautious, for he wanted to take his opponent's measure, so to speak.

Sure of victory, the bully rushed at him, and aimed a blow at Mont's nose.

Our hero ducked, and Hoke's fist only sawed the air.

"That was a clean duck."

"Land him one, Hoke!"

"Go for him, Folsom!"

Around and around the ring went the two boys.

Then the bully aimed another blow at our hero.

As quick as a flash our hero warded it off.

Then out shot his fist, and the bully of Nautical Hall got a crashing blow in the chin that knocked him clean off his feet.

What a yell went up!

"Hoke is knocked out!"

"Did you ever see such a blow?"

Wild with rage, the bully was assisted to his feet by several friends.

The blood flowed from his chin and from a cut lip.

"I'll show you yet!" he hissed, and again went at Mont.

But our hero was cool and collected, while the bully was excited.

The bully got in one little body blow, but that was all, while our hero fairly played all over his face.

"Better give it up, Hoke!"

"You are outclassed against Mont Folsom!"

"Let me be!" howled the bully.

With every blow that our hero delivered Ummer's anger increased.

His reputation, he felt, was at stake.

If he was beaten that would be the end of him, so far as bossing the boys was concerned.

At last Mont hit him a stinging blow on the ear that caused him to roll over and over.

CHAPTER IV

ON THE ROAD

The bully was knocked out completely, and had to acknowledge Mont the victor of the encounter.

This he did with very bad grace, and a minute later sneaked off with his toady.

"I'll get even for that," he growled. "He'll be sorry he ever tackled me."

"You'll have to watch Hoke Ummer," said Link, some time later, when the crowd had dispersed. "He is a treacherous fellow."

"I'll have my eyes open," returned our hero.

Yet little did he dream of the dastardly way in which the bully would try to get even.

It did not take Mont long to settle down at Nautical Hall. The fight had made him many friends, and established him as a sort of leader among a certain set.

On the following Saturday Link proposed that he, Barry

Powell, and Mont take a stroll down to the village.

The others were willing, and soon the party was on the way.

"I'll get some stuff for a midnight feast while I am at it," said Mont.

Soon the school was left behind, and they came out on the village highway.

"Hark!" cried Barry suddenly.

"What is it?" demanded Mont.

Barry was listening intently to a dull, heavy tramping sound, which was wafted faintly toward them on the breeze.

"Do you hear that?" he asked excitedly.

Link and Mont listened, and could distinctly hear a low thud, thud, thud in the distance.

"What does it mean?" Link asked.

"It means that a pair of ponies, or horses, have run away, and are coming along at a tearing gallop."

As if in corroboration of Barry's words, at that moment a light phaeton, drawn by two high-spirited ponies, which were pounding along at the top of their speed, burst round the bend of the road.

The vehicle was rocking from side to side, and every moment threatened to hurl it into one of the deep ditches which lined the road.

As the boys gazed at the approaching carriage Mont's heart seemed to stand still.

"Fellows!" he cried, "there is someone in the phaeton—a lady, I believe."

"So there is!" gasped Link, in tones of horror. "What shall we do?"

"We must stop them."

With his face whiter than usual, and his lips tightly compressed, our hero ran down the road.

"He is courting death," said his chum, beneath his breath, "but we may be of some use."

And both started after their companion.

Mont was running at the top of his speed, for he saw that the occupant of the carriage was only a young girl, and utterly helpless, and that every second's delay endangered her life.

On and on he went, until he was within a score of yards of the maddened steeds.

Then he planted himself firmly in the middle of the road and prepared for a spring.

Fiercely the ponies dashed onward.

Nearer and nearer they came, until it seemed they must inevitably trample him beneath their iron-shod hoofs.

But our hero never wavered.

Motionless he crouched there until the end of the pole almost touched his cheek.

Then he leaped up and caught both the bridles in his strong, nervous grip.

The ponies, with loud whinnies of rage, tossed up their heads and lifted him from his feet, but he clung tenaciously to them.

They dragged him along the ground for a few yards, and then their speed began to slacken.

Link now came up, and the vicious little brutes were brought to a standstill.

Then Mont, thoroughly exhausted, sank in a heap upon the ground.

As soon as the carriage was stopped in its wild career, a fair and beautiful girl sprang out.

"Oh, is he very much hurt?" she cried, as she raised her clasped hands in despair.

Our hero staggered to his feet, and as he gazed on the fairy-like form and sweet, delicate face his cheeks flushed and his heart beat quickly.

"I am not hurt at all," he said stoutly, although his arms and legs and every portion of his body ached as though he had been upon the rack.

"How can I thank you?" she exclaimed. "If it had not been for you, I shudder to think what might have happened. You saved my life."

At this praise our hero blushed more than ever.

"I require no thanks," he said. "I am rewarded enough by knowing I have been of some service to you, but I think you are scarcely strong enough to be trusted with such high-spirited animals."

"My father would never have thought of such a thing," she replied. "He alighted at a cottage to visit one of his old friends, and while he was inside the ponies bolted. But here he comes, and I know he will be better able to thank you than I am."

She pointed to the figure of a tall, elderly gentleman, of upright carriage and aristocratic bearing, who was coming up the road at a rapid pace.

"It's Judge Moore," whispered Link; "he owns a fine place a couple of miles from here."

In another moment our hero found himself being presented to the judge, who overwhelmed him with praise.

"You must come and dine with us, you and your friends," said the judge; "there will only be myself and my daughter Alice. Nay, you must make no excuses. I shall call upon Captain Hooper and tell him all about it, and if ever you require a friend do not forget to come to me."

Mont would have respectfully declined the invitation, but a glance from Alice Moore prevented him from doing so.

He therefore thanked the judge for his kindness, and then the boys took their leave.

Our hero simply raised his cap, but Alice put out her hand.

"You will be certain to come?" she asked in a low tone.

"Certain," he replied.

The news of Mont's heroism spread through Nautical Hall, and he speedily found himself a decided hero.

CHAPTER V

HOKE UMMER'S TREACHERY

Our hero succeeded on the following Monday in getting a quantity of cake, pie, and other stuff from town and hiding them in an unoccupied bedroom.

He was also promised a dozen bottles of root beer and soda water, but these he was unable to smuggle into the school, owing to the watchfulness of Captain Hooper and his assistants.

Accordingly, he hid the stuff in the bushes near the lake, and decided to go after it late at night.

He unfolded his plan to Link, Barry, and Carl Barnaby, and this plan was overheard by Hoke Ummer.

Next to the empty bedroom was a window overlooking the side playground. From this window Mont decided to reach the ground by aid of a long rope.

This was the only way to get out, as after nine o'clock all the doors and windows below were locked in such a fashion they could not be opened.

Roy Rockwood

That evening our hero, with a light heart, repaired to the empty bedroom.

Opening the boxful of stuff, he spread out upon a tablecloth of newspapers a prettily decorated ham, a couple of cold roast chickens, a fine apple pie, a quantity of mince pies, and a varied assortment of choice fruits and cake.

All these arranged to his satisfaction, he looked at his watch, and then sat down and waited.

It was just half-past eight, and in another half-hour servants and masters would all have retired for the night.

After what appeared to the watcher to be an age the great school clock tolled solemnly out the hour of nine.

Then Mont drew out a thick rope from beneath the bed and left the room.

Soon he was at the window.

Throwing up the lower sash, our hero fastened one end of the rope securely and threw the other out.

"Just the right length," he said, and then he swung himself over the window sill. "I'll soon have the rest of the stuff up."

The door of one of the spare bedrooms was opened, and Ummer stepped into the corridor.

As the light of the moon fell upon his face it looked strangely white and ghastly.

His lips were tightly compressed and his eyes had in them a horrible glare as he stepped stealthily but quickly to the window.

Arrived there, he crouched low down that he might not be seen by any person outside.

Then, with deft fingers, he untied the knot by which the rope was secured.

There was heard a loud, wild cry, followed by a dull, heavy thud.

Then all was still.

The bully crept away along the corridor and down the stairs, his heart beating as though it would burst its bounds.

A little before twelve o'clock that night several dark figures might have been seen stealing cautiously along the corridors.

All these figures made their way to one common spot.

This was the bedroom Mont had mentioned.

Arrived there, they found everything prepared for the feast, but no host.

"What a strange thing for Mont to do," said Carl Barnaby; "to invite us all here and not be present."

"It isn't very gentlemanly of him," submitted Barry.

"You talk like a fool," said Link. "Something must have happened to him."

"I saw him at supper, and he was all right then."

"Perhaps some of the tramps have waylaid him on the road," suggested another boy, who had been sitting very white and very quiet, in one corner of the room.

Everyone turned to the speaker.

"Mine cracious, dot's so," put in Sam Schump. "Besser we go an' see?"

Without delay a search was begun.

A rope was procured, and Link was the first person out of the window.

"Hullo!"

"What's up?" asked those above.

"Bring a light. Mont has fallen and hurt himself."

A light was quickly procured, and one after another the boys came down the rope.

Our hero lay at the foot of a large lilac bush.

It was this bush which had saved his life.

When the rope gave way, had he fallen on the ground he would most likely have been killed.

Link brought some water, and he was soon revived.

In the meantime, from another window, overhead, Hoke Ummer watched proceedings.

When he saw Mont get up his hateful face plainly showed

his chagrin.

"How was it you didn't fasten the rope tightly?" asked Link.

"I thought I did," returned our hero. "In fact, I am certain I did," he added.

"But it gave way and let you down."

Our hero shook his head. He couldn't understand it at all.

In a few minutes he was able to go with his friends and show them where the root-beer and soda-water bottles were hidden.

Loaded down with the stuff, the crowd returned to the Hall, and the feast began.

Nearly all of the boys of Mont's age had been invited in a general way, and a lively time was had for fully an hour.

Hoke Ummer could not stand it to see his rival triumph over him, and so slipped down to the room occupied by Moses Sparks, one of the under teachers.

"Mont Folsom and his crowd are having a feast in one of the upper rooms," he said.

At once Moses Sparks prepared to investigate.

The feast was at its height when a footstep was heard.

"Scatter!" whispered Carl Barnaby, who caught the sounds first, and all of the boys hurried from the bedroom by side doors and managed to get to their own rooms.

When Moses Sparks came up they seemed to be sleeping like so many lambs.

"Ummer has been fooling me," muttered the under teacher. "Or else he was mistaken." And he went off and left the boys to finish the feast in peace.

CHAPTER VI

OUT ON THE BAY

In a general way Mont suspected Hoke Ummer, not of the dastardly trick he had played, but of playing the sneak and telling Moses Sparks.

"I'll get square," he said to Link and Carl.

Out in the fields he had picked up a dead snake, and he now resolved to make use of it in a truly original manner. As soon as it was time to retire that night Mont slipped upstairs and into the dormitory occupied by Hoke Ummer, Goul, and their chums.

He had the dead snake with him, and put the reptile in the bully's bed.

Five minutes later he was in his own room awaiting developments.

They were not long in coming.

A murmur of voices ended in a wild shriek of terror.

"A snake!" yelled Hoke. "It's in my bed! Save me! I'm a

Roy Rockwood

dead boy!"

His cry aroused everyone, and soon Nautical Hall was in a commotion.

"What's the matter with Hoke?"

"He's got 'em bad!"

"A snake!" roared the bully. "Take it away."

He ran out into the corridor, and soon a crowd began to collect.

In the meantime Mont slipped into the room and threw the dead reptile out of the window.

Captain Hooper tried to get at the bottom of the affair, but failed.

"You must have been dreaming, Ummer," he said at last, and sent all of the boys off to bed.

During the following week Nautical Hall was closed up, and the schoolboy cadets marched to the head of the bay.

Here they went into camp for a month, part of the time being spent on the bay and the ocean beyond in learning how to sail both large and small boats.

The sailing of the boats particularly interested Mont and Carl Barnaby. Link did not care very much for the water, for when the sea was rough he was inclined to grow seasick.

One day Mont and Carl obtained permission to hire a sloop at the town, and go out for an all-day cruise over the bay and back.

They took with them a young fellow from Nautical Hall named John Stumpton, a handy lad who generally went by the name of Stump. Since Mont had arrived at the Hall, Stump had taken to him greatly, and would do almost anything that Mont asked of him. Stump was also a great friend to Carl.

They sailed out of sight of the camp, and gradually crept up to a large excursion boat which was just leaving one of the docks of the town.

The steamboat was overcrowded, every deck being full of humanity bent on having a good time.

Some musicians were playing on the forward deck, and they drew quite close to hear what was going on.

Suddenly a cry of horror arose.

A young girl had been standing close to the rail on a camp chair at the bow of the boat.

It was Alice Moore.

As the steamboat swung around the girl lost her balance.

She tried to save herself, and, failing, pitched headlong into the water.

Our hero saw her go under the waves.

"She'll be struck by the paddle wheel," he yelled, and then, splash! he was overboard himself.

Bravely he struck out to save the maiden.

The order was given to back the steamboat.

The wheels churned up the water into a white foam, but still the momentum carried the large craft on.

In the meantime our hero came up and struck out valiantly for the girl, who was now going down for a second time.

"Save her! Save her!" shrieked Judge Moore, who was with his daughter.

Half a dozen life-preservers were thrown overboard, but none came to where the girl could reach them.

The judge wanted to join his daughter in the water.

Strong hands held him back.

"The young fellow will save her, judge."

"He's a true hero!"

Life-lines were thrown over, but even these did no good.

The steamboat swung around, but the run of the water washed the girl closer and closer to the paddle wheel.

She now came up a second time.

Should she sink again all would be over.

Mont was swimming with all the strength and skill at his command.

At last he was within a yard of the struggling girl.

The maiden threw up her hands and went under. As quick as a flash our hero dove down.

A second passed. Then up came our hero with the girl clinging to his shoulder.

But now the current was apparently too strong for both of them.

"Help us—quick!"

Carl and Stump heard the cry, and immediately put about in their sloop.

Mont was swimming along on his side.

The girl was too weak to support herself, and he was holding her up well out of the water.

It took the sloop but a moment to run up alongside of the pair.

Carl reached over and caught hold of the girl and placed her on deck.

In the meantime our hero caught hold of a rope thrown by the old boatman and pulled himself up.

A cheer arose from those on the excursion boat.

"She is safe now, sure!"

The girl was too exhausted to move, and Carl rubbed her hands and did what he could for her.

Stump ran up alongside of the steamboat, and a little later the girl was placed on board.

The judge clasped his child to his breast.

"Go ahead," said Mont in a low voice. "I don't want the crowd to stare at me."

"But the judge wants to thank you," began Carl; but our hero would not listen.

He was too modest, and made Stump actually run away from the excursion boat.

But five hundred people cheered Mont and waved their handkerchiefs.

And this was not the end of the matter.

The next day Judge Moore called at the camp, and insisted on presenting Mont with a gold watch and chain. With this gift came a sweet letter from Alice Moore which made our hero blush a good deal when he read it.

After this, nearly a week passed without special incident. Link was called home on account of the death of a relative, and Mont and Carl became closer chums than ever.

One day Hoke Ummer was caught abusing one of the small boys so greatly that the boy had to be placed under a doctor's care.

The boy's father had Hoke arrested. The case, however, never came to trial.

The consequence of the arrest was that the bully was

dismissed from the school; and that was the last Mont saw of him.

"We are well rid of him," he said, and Carl and the others agreed with him.

One day Mont and Carl went out for an all-day cruise on the bay, taking John Stumpton with them.

When the two schoolboys started out with the hired lad they did not intend to remain away longer than sunset, and not one of them dreamed of the marvelous adventures in store for each ere he should be permitted to see his native land again.

The start was made in a fair breeze, and it looked so nice overhead that Mont proposed they take a short run directly into the ocean.

"All right—I'll go you," answered Carl slangily, and away they skimmed.

By noon they were almost out of sight of land, and while they were eating the repast Stump had prepared Carl proposed that they turn back.

This was hardly accomplished when it suddenly grew dark, and they found themselves caught in a squall.

"By gracious! I didn't bargain for this!" cried Carl. "If we don't take care, we'll go to the bottom!"

"Don't worry—yet," answered Mont. "I guess we'll get back all right."

Blacker and blacker grew the sky, until absolutely nothing

could be seen. Every sail was closely reefed, and the boys strained their eyes to pierce the gloom which hung over them.

Suddenly Stump set up a yell.

"Look out; there is a ship!"

He got no further. A large form loomed up in the darkness. There was one grinding, smashing crash, and then came a shock that split the light-built sloop from stem to stern.

All of the boys were hurled into the boiling sea. But none was hurt; and, coming to the surface, all struggled to cling to the wreckage floating about, meanwhile crying loudly for help.

When they were picked up they were thoroughly exhausted, and Carl lost his senses completely.

The ship that had run them down was the *Golden Cross*. The captain's name was Savage, and he was bound for the Bermudas.

He refused to stop anywhere to put the boys off, saying he had not the time to do so.

In reality he was afraid he would be brought to account for wrecking the sloop.

He would not believe that Mont and Carl were rich, and that their parents would willingly pay him for any trouble he might take on their behalf.

"I'll keep 'em on board and make 'em work their passage," he said to his mate, a mean chap by the name of Slog. "We are rather short of hands."

A night's rest did wonders for the boys.

By morning the storm cleared off, and the *Golden Cross* proceeded swiftly on her way, favored by a good breeze.

Mont found himself in the ill-smelling forecastle. He was awfully hungry, and the first thing he did was to make his way to the cook's galley. The cook smiled as Mont appeared. "Got around, eh?" he said. "Good for you. I thought you would be sick for the rest of the trip after such an adventure."

"I am pretty tough," answered Mont.

"You look a bit like a sailor."

"Oh, I know a thing or two about the water," replied Mont modestly. "But tell me," he went on, "what sort of a captain have you?"

"Oh, he's a caution, and so is Slog, the first mate," laughed the cook. "The captain is the toughest man this line of ships ever had."

"Humph! That's not encouraging," mused our hero. "Why do the owners keep him?"

"Because he's clever. He may be out in all weather, but he's never lost a ship."

"This seems like an old tub," observed Mont, looking around him.

"Yes, she isn't worth much. She pitches and tosses in a gale awful. It's the oldest ship the firm's got."

"Is it insured?"

"Yes. I know the insurance is very heavy, and it wouldn't be a bad job for the owners if she went down," replied the cook.

"Bad job for us, though," remarked Mont. "I don't want to be drowned."

"Have you had any breakfast?" asked the cook good-naturedly.

"Not a bit."

"I don't expect the regular hands will give you a chance of getting much. There's Sam Holly and Jerry Dabble. One's a bully and the other's a sneak."

"I haven't seen them yet."

"Fight shy of both of them. They're no good. They'll make you and your chums do all the work, now you've come on board."

"I'll bet a dollar they won't get a stroke of work out of me," returned Mont decidedly.

"You will?"

"Yes."

"Well, you're a plucky lad," exclaimed the cook admiringly, "and from your size and looks I should think you could box."

"Just a little bit," answered Mont smilingly.

"The captain favors Jerry Dabble, and listens to all he says.

He's a regular sneak. You look out for him."

"I will."

"Will you have a bit of breakfast along with me? I can give you a nice bit I've cut off the skipper's ham and a couple of eggs."

"I'm with you," said Mont readily, "and I'll return your kindness on the first opportunity."

In a moment our hero was supplied with a good breakfast, which was washed down with a cup of coffee.

The sea was rather high, although the wind had gone down.

It was not difficult to perceive, when Mont came to examine her, that the ship was a very old one and had seen her best days.

Mont thought a trip to the Bermudas would be very nice, but at the same time he did not mean to be the captain's slave, or the first mate's either.

He had not shipped with them, and they could not legally make him work, though he did not mind lending a hand if he was asked in a friendly manner.

His mother would pay for his passage if she was asked.

The officers evidently took him, Carl, and Stump to be three sons of fishermen, and had made up their minds to treat them accordingly.

When he left the galley, Mont went to where the regular hands slept and messed, and where he and his companions had slept.

There was a great outcry as he came in.

"Leave off, I say," Carl was exclaiming; "I won't have it. Two of you onto me at once isn't fair."

In a moment Mont was there. He found the two young men, Sam Holly and Jerry Dabble, standing over his chum with two ropes' ends, with which they were hitting him.

"What are you licking him for?" asked Mont, his eyes flashing.

"Because he won't get the breakfast," said Holly.

"He's not your servant—why should he?"

"He'll have to do it, or you will," said Sam the bully, setting his arms akimbo and staring impudently at Mont.

"My good fellow," said the latter, "don't you make any error. Neither my friend nor myself means to do anything on board this ship unless we're asked civilly."

Jerry Dabble laughed. "You're a fool to talk that way!" he roared.

Mont immediately gave him a cuff on the ears which sent him rolling over a bunk.

CHAPTER VII

A LIVELY ENCOUNTER

The two sailors were astonished beyond measure at Mont's quick action.

"Good for you, Mont!" cried Carl Barnaby, while Stump grinned with intense delight.

"I'll go and tell the captain," growled Jerry, as he got up slowly.

Sam Holly, who was a thick-set, heavy-looking fellow, turned to Mont. "I have had enough of this nonsense. Do you mean to do your work or not?"

"Certainly not; do it yourself."

"Do you want a good hiding?"

"You can't give it to me."

"I can try, can't I?" said Holly.

"So can any other fool; but it doesn't follow he will do it."

"Look here, I've been two voyages before this. You're a green hand compared to me, and I'm boss here. We are short-handed. Do the work, and I'll make things easy for you; if not, it will be worse for you."

"I'll chance that," said Mont.

"Do you mean to risk a sound thrashing?"

"Oh, yes, I'm game for a rough-and-tumble. It's sure to come sooner or later, and we may as well get it over at once."

"Mind your eye, then," yelled Holly.

His ugly face glowed with passion, and his great, stupid-looking ears seemed to stick out like cabbage leaves.

"Come on," he said.

"I'm ready," returned Mont.

The fight commenced in the little cabin, and it was evident that the combatants were in earnest.

Our hero found his opponent as strong as a young bull, but he had not very much skill.

Parrying his blows and hitting hard when he had a good chance, Mont punished him severely.

But he was knocked down first.

"Will that do for you," said Holly, "or do you want any more?"

"More, please," exclaimed Mont, getting up. And then he

clipped Holly two heavy ones that knocked him nearly down a ladder.

Holly foamed with rage. "Come on!" he exclaimed, in a husky voice.

The fight continued for ten minutes, with varying success. At last Mont saw a good chance, and, pretending to strike Holly's face, he dropped his hand and hit him in the stomach.

As the bully fell back, gasping for breath, Mont exclaimed:

"How do you like it now, you bully? Do you want any more?"

"Not this voyage," rejoined Holly dismally; "you're best man."

"It's a pity you didn't find that out before," remarked Mont. "However, it's never too late to learn. Perhaps you will get our breakfast ready. I'm master now. Do you understand that, Mr. Bully?"

"Don't crow. I'm licked this time, but my turn may come. Sit down and have your grub."

Mont was quite satisfied with his victory.

He shook hands with Holly, and they all sat down together, making a comfortable breakfast, though the fare was not luxurious.

Carl and our hero went on deck afterward, and, hearing an altercation forward, ran in that direction.

Captain Savage was beating a sailor with a marlinspike for

some breach of discipline.

The crew looked on without interfering.

The sailor was a fine, handsome fellow, and in vain begged the tyrant to desist. The poor fellow's face was streaming with blood, and Mont's anger arose instantly.

Rushing forward, he seized the captain's arm, and exclaimed:

"Stop that—I won't have it!"

The next moment he was alarmed at his rashness.

Turning upon him with incredible fury, the captain exclaimed:

"How dare you speak to me, youngster! I'll break every bone in your body!"

At a sign from the first mate, on whose face sat a smile of malicious satisfaction, four men fell upon Mont, whose arms were pinioned, and he was thrown on his back, where he lay perfectly helpless.

"Take him away," continued Captain Savage. "I will deal with him presently. It's a pity I took the young whelp on board; he should have drowned if I'd have known what he was made of."

Strong arms lifted Mont up, and he was forced into a dark hole, near the cook's galley, where he was half stifled with the heat and smell of tar.

Mont felt he was now in for it, and no mistake.

CHAPTER VIII

MONT IS PUNISHED

"Hang the luck, anyway!"

In a miserable state of mind, but still very angry, Mont sat down in his gloomy prison, and wondered what would happen next.

An hour later the captain called up the first mate.

"Let the prisoner be brought forward, and call the hands to witness punishment; muster them all. I mean to make an example."

The mate summoned the crew, all of whom trooped forward with a sullen and discontented air.

The first mate went to Mont, and personally conducted him on deck.

"Now, my lad," said the captain, with a brutal air, "I'm going to let you know what discipline is. Strip!"

Looking around him defiantly, Mont did not move.

"Do you hear me?" thundered the captain. "Strip!"

"Captain Savage," said Mont quietly, "I protest against this treatment. You saved my life and the lives of my companions, for which I thank you. We would leave your ship at once if we could. As it is, we are unwilling passengers."

"You are a part of the crew, and must work out your passage."

"Not at all. We have not signed articles, and you have no power over us so long as we conduct ourselves properly."

"Why did you interfere between me and one of my crew? But I'll waste no words with you," replied the captain. "Tie him to the foremast."

He caught up the rope's end and hit Mont a single blow.

He was about to go on, when the sailors advanced in a body, and formed a line between him and Mont.

"Back, you scoundrels! Back, mutinous dogs!" exclaimed the captain in a greater rage than ever.

The solid line remained immovable, and Mont was set free.

Both mates put themselves by the captain's side, as they feared a crisis was approaching, and they determined to side with the skipper.

"Look'ee here, cappen," said an old, grizzled sailor. "I've shipped aboard o' many vessels, and I've seen a few skippers, but never the likes o' you. We don't want to do you no harm, but we aint a-goin' to stan' by and see that poor lad flogged half to death because he interfered for one o' us."

"I'll have you all tried at the first port I come to!" exclaimed the captain.

Slog, the mate, caught the captain's arm.

"For Heaven's sake, go below, and leave them to me!" he said.

"Not I. Where are my pistols? I'll shoot some of the dogs."

"Be guided by me, sir. Let them alone this time, and tackle them one by one. If you don't, they'll do something desperate."

The captain mumbled something which was inaudible. He was almost speechless with rage.

Suddenly the voice of the lookout man rang out clearly:

"A strange sail."

"Where away?" asked the captain.

"On the larboard bow, sir."

The captain took his telescope, and began to examine the strange sail.

Everyone crowded to the side to have a look, and every eye was soon searching the horizon.

Even Mont shared the excitement.

He had a pocket glass, and brought it into use.

"Perhaps we'll be taken off," he said to Carl.

"I sincerely hope so," replied his chum. "I've had enough of this ship."

CHAPTER IX

DOCTOR HOMER WODDLE

It was soon discovered that the sail was nothing more or less than a man clinging to a chicken coop, who had taken off his shirt and hoisted it on high to attract attention.

When he was neared, a boat was lowered, and the unfortunate man picked up and brought on board.

He was a little, wiry man, about forty-five years of age, with sharp, intelligent face, and an expression of anything but good temper.

"Which is the captain of this vessel?" he asked on coming aboard.

"I am," replied Captain Savage.

"You've been a long time picking me up. What do you mean by it?" said the little man.

"That's a cool remark," said the captain, "considering we have, in all probability, saved your life."

"And if you have, you only did your duty. Where is your

cabin? Give me some fresh clothes immediately, and something to eat and drink."

"You've got a nerve," said the captain, inclined to be angry.
"I've a good mind never to save anyone again."

"That will not matter much to me. You are not likely to save
me twice."

"Who are you?"

"My name is Homer Woddle, sir."

"You speak loud enough," replied the captain.

"Bah! it's evident you are not a man of science, or you would
have heard of me. I have written books, sir—books!"

"What then?"

"I am a famous man. My position in life is that of Secretary
to the Society for the Exploration of the Unknown Parts of
the World, sir, and I am making my third voyage."

"How were you wrecked?"

"That is the strangest thing. But give me to eat and drink,
clothe me, and you shall hear."

"Speak first, and then I'll think of it, Mr. Woddle," said the
captain.

The conversation was audible enough to be heard by all on
board, who crowded round the speakers in a way that
showed how severely discipline on board the ship had been
interfered with by the late occurrence.

"Well, well, well," cried the little man, irritably, "what a boy you are! I left Boston last week on board the *Comet*. Well, sir, that ship was fitted up at a great expense in order that we might make discoveries. Do you see?"

"Not clearly as yet," answered the captain.

"Tush, be quiet," exclaimed the irritable little man; "don't interrupt me. This morning about eight o'clock we were struck amidships, but below the water line, by a wonderful sea monster, which nearly cut us in two."

"Did the ship sink?"

"She did almost directly afterward. I seized a chicken coop, and here I am."

"A monster cut you in two!" exclaimed the captain, opening his eyes. "What sort of a monster? Did you see it?"

"We did for a few minutes. It was black and long, like a gigantic eel, and threw out phosphorescent light."

"Then there was something electric about it?" remarked the first mate.

"Undoubtedly."

"That's a strange yarn," observed the captain.

He took Dr. Homer Woddle, the Secretary of the Society for the Exploration of the Unknown Parts of the World, into his cabin, gave him dry clothes, and provided him with the best dinner the resources of the ship could afford.

Mont had listened curiously to the conversation between

Captain Savage and the newcomer.

Taking Carl's arm, he said:

"That's a wonderful yarn of that fellow who has just come on board."

"Very."

"I don't know what to make of it, exactly. A fish is a fish, and unless it has a big horn, it can't sink a ship."

"Perhaps he's cracked."

"Not he. I have heard of him. There is something in it. The man is sane enough. He has been wrecked, and he has told his story plainly enough, only I don't believe in the strange animal."

"What is it, then?"

"That's the mystery. There can't be any rocks in the middle of the sea. It isn't a rock."

"Then it must be a wonderful fish."

A couple of hours passed when Dr. Woddle came on deck, arm in arm with Captain Savage.

After a time the scientist left the captain, and met Mont.

"Nice weather, my lad," he exclaimed.

"Who are you calling 'my lad'?" asked Mont.

"You're one of the crew, I suppose, and you needn't be

so snappish."

"I'm a passenger," replied Mont, "and my name is Mont Folsom. Sorry I haven't got a card, but I was wrecked yesterday, and that will account for it. I and my companions come from Nautical Hall."

"Indeed! I presume you were picked up as I was? Did you meet with the singular animal that destroyed my ship?"

"Can't say I did. What was he like?"

"A huge, long thing, covered with scales, half in, half out of the water."

"Are we likely to meet with him again?"

"I should think so," answered the scientist. "Look there!"

"Where?" exclaimed Mont.

"To the right. I don't understand those confounded sea terms, and I don't know larboard from starboard, but on my right is the creature."

"The dreaded animal?" asked Mont, with a laugh.

"Yes. Look!"

Our hero followed the direction of the outstretched arm, and beheld a curious sight.

Not far from the ship was a long, black-looking thing, lying like a great round log on the water.

It was the submarine monster.

CHAPTER X

THE SUBMARINE TERROR

Captain Savage at once came to the rail, and was soon busily engaged in looking at the wonderful creature which Homer Woddle declared had sunk the ship in which he had been sailing.

The crew were much agitated, for seamen are at all times superstitious, and, never having heard of such a strange monster, they fancied its appearance boded no good.

The monster, which had been perfectly inert up to this time, threw out a marvelous light, which illuminated the depths of the sea.

The magnificent irradiation was evidently the result of electricity, and it revealed the shape of the strange fish, if fish it was, very distinctly.

Its form was what we may call a lengthened oval, tapering off at the head and tail, which were under the water, only part of the scaly back being exposed to the air.

Dr. Woddle called the captain.

"Sir," he said, "the monster is again close to us. I ask you, in the interest of science, to capture it."

"Who's going to do it, and how is it to be done?" said Captain Savage.

"This thing is a scourge of the ocean. It destroys ships, therefore it is your duty to destroy it," persisted the man of science.

"We will harpoon it, if you like, though I do not know why I should risk the lives of my crew. Where's Bowline? Pass the word for Bowline," said the captain.

When Bill Bowline made his appearance he was trembling like a leaf.

"Get your harpoon, my man," said the captain.

"Not me, sir," said the sailor firmly. "I wouldn't harm a scale of the critter's back, were it ever so near. We shall all be sent to the bottom of the sea if I do."

Turning to Homer Woddle, the captain said:

"You see the feeling of my men; what can I do?"

"I'll do it myself," said the man of science grandly. "If no one will attack this monster, the honor and the glory of the task shall belong to me. Give me a boat and loaded guns. It will be hard, indeed, if I cannot put a bullet in him, and lay the mighty brute low. Who will volunteer for this splendid task?"

There was no response.

"What! Are you all cowards? Will no one volunteer?" continued the man of science scornfully.

Mont stepped forward.

"I'm with you, sir!" he exclaimed. "Can't stand by and see a gentleman left alone. I'm not afraid of the creature."

Carl, as a matter of course, took his place by our hero's side, and so did Stump.

Where Mont went his devoted friend and equally attached follower felt bound to go as a matter of duty.

"Three of you. Bravo!" cried the scientist. "Now, we are four, and we shall triumph. Lower a boat, if you please."

The order was given to put the ship about, and a spot favorable for the enterprise being selected near the monster, a boat was lowered, into which the volunteers descended.

Carl and Stump took the oars, Mont grasped the tiller, and Dr. Woddle stood in the bows with a loaded gun under each arm.

"My four troublesome customers," said the captain, in a low tone to the first mate, "stand a very good chance of never returning."

"It will be a cheap way to get rid of them, although it may cost us the boat," said the mate in the same tone.

"Steady, my lads," said the scientist. "Easy all; keep the head before the wind, Mr. Folsom, if you please."

"Steady she is," answered Mont.

The boat stopped at a short distance from the monster, and Homer Woddle stood up, placed a gun to his shoulder, and fired.

The ball struck the huge slumbering beast, but glided off its back as if it had struck a piece of polished steel.

"Hard as the hide of a rhinoceros," said the man of science; "we must try again. Steady, boys."

The monster, however, did not seem to approve of being shot at, and seemed to tremble violently for a moment.

Then with incredible velocity it darted past the rowboat, which was upset in a moment, and proceeded to strike the ship.

It struck the unfortunate vessel a terrific blow directly back of the bow.

The crash was distinctly audible, and amid the noise of falling masts and flapping sails were heard the cries of the sailors and the moans of the dying.

After the concussion the monster retired as it had come.

A cloud obscured the surface of the ocean, and it was difficult to tell where it had gone, or what had become of the ship.

Mont found himself struggling in the sea, and wondered what had become of his companions.

"Hang those monsters of the deep," he said to himself; "I don't like them."

Swimming gently, he got hold of one of the oars of the boat, and so kept himself afloat without much exertion.

It was not a hopeful position to be in.

Struggling alone in the middle of a vast ocean, ignorant of the fate of his companions, and doubtful of succor, it was not to be wondered at if he felt inclined to despair.

Would he sink or swim? The question was, just then, a hard one to answer.

CHAPTER XI

ON THE BACK OF THE MONSTER

Mont was alone on the ocean with nothing but water in sight.

Yet his heart did not fail him.

"Well," he said aloud, "I like adventures, and now I have met with a beautiful one. Perhaps I shall be picked up. Perhaps not."

Five minutes passed. To our hero they seemed an age.

"Hullo! Hi! What cheer? Ship ahoy!" he cried.

He had scarcely closed his lips, after this appeal for help, when he felt his arm seized vigorously.

"Who are you?" he asked.

"If you will lean upon my shoulder," was the reply, "you will soon gain strength and swim better."

"Is it you, Stump?" said Mont, recognizing the voice of his faithful friend.

"At your service, Master Mont. I have been swimming about everywhere looking for you ever since that submarine beast swamped us. Ugh! What a terrible brute it is! It laughs at bullets, and cares no more for sinking a ship than I should for kicking over a stool."

"Is no one saved?"

"I can't tell any more than you; all I thought of was to swim after you."

The situation was as terrible a one as can well be imagined.

Those on board the vessel were in too much trouble, if they were yet living, to think of the perils of the others who had courted destruction by going in the boat to attack the monster.

Nor would Captain Savage feel very friendly disposed toward them, because it was Dr. Woddle's shot that caused the slumbering creature to rush madly upon the vessel.

Mont began to calculate the chances of safety. If the ship had not foundered the crew might lower another boat in the morning to search for them. The sun would not rise for about eight hours. Could they exist so long in the water without fainting or becoming cramped by the sluggish circulation of the blood?

In vain he tried to pierce the dense darkness which surrounded them, for now the moon had disappeared, and bad weather seemed imminent again.

About two o'clock in the morning our hero was seized with extreme fatigue; his limbs were a prey to an agonizing cramp.

Stump put his arm around him, but he drew his breath with difficulty, and evidently required all his strength for himself.

"Let me go, boy," said Mont; "save yourself."

"Certainly not," said Stump quickly. "We're not going down just yet."

At that moment the moon appeared again from under the edge of a thick cloud which had concealed it for a time, and the surface of the sea sparkled under its rays.

This fortunate light put new strength into the boys, and Mont searched the horizon with eager, careful gaze.

He saw the ship, or what appeared to be her, about two miles off, looking like a somber, inert mass, but there was no sign of a boat.

At first he was inclined to cry for help, but of what use would it have been at that distance?

"Here, this way! Hi! help, help!" shouted Stump.

Was it one of those delusive sounds which the anxious mind sometimes conjures up, or did an answer really come to the lad's cry for help?

"Did you hear anything?" asked Mont.

"Yes, I thought so," said Stump, and he began to cry out again.

"Help, help!"

This time there was no mistake. A human voice clearly

responded through the darkness.

Stump lifted himself as high out of the water as he could, and taking a look, fell back exhausted, clinging desperately to the oar.

"Did you see anything?" asked Mont anxiously.

"Yes; don't talk, sir; we want all our strength."

There was a hopeful ring in his voice which inspired Mont, who, however, fancied he heard the boy sigh almost directly afterward.

He thought of the monster. Was it still near them? But, if so, whence came the voice?

They began to swim with all the strength they had left, and after some minutes of continued exertion, for moving was a painful task in their state, Stump spoke again.

"Are you far off?" he said.

"Not far—push on," replied the voice, which Mont fancied he knew.

Suddenly an outstretched hand seized him; he was pulled violently out of the water, just as his senses were going, and, after someone had rubbed his hands vigorously, he opened his eyes and murmured:

"Stump."

"Here, sir," replied the lad.

By the rays of the moon our hero saw a figure which was not

that of Stump, but which he recognized easily.

"Dr. Woddle?" he said.

"Right, my lad," answered the man of science.

"Where is Carl?"

"Here," answered our hero's chum. "The doctor and I stuck together, and our only concern has been for you."

"Where are we?" asked Mont puzzled; "this thing I am sitting on seems firm enough."

"It's a floating island," answered Woddle.

A horrible thought crossed Mont's mind to which he could not give expression.

"To put you out of your misery at once," continued Dr. Woddle, "we are on the back of the gigantic creature at whom I shot, and I know now why I did not kill him."

"Why?"

"Because he is ironclad, or something very like it. I can make no impression upon the scaly monster with my knife."

These words produced a strange feeling in Mont's mind. He found that he was really with his friends on the back of the monster, which continued to float on the surface, after causing the partial destruction of the ship.

He got up and stamped his foot. It was certainly a hard, impenetrable body, and not the soft substance of which all the marine inhabitants that he had heard of were made, such as whales, sharks, walruses, and the like. If anything, it more resembled a tortoise or an alligator. A hollow sound was emitted when it was struck, and it appeared to be made of cast-iron plates secured together.

"What is your opinion of the creature, sir?" asked Mont.

"You want my candid opinion as a man of science?" said the doctor.

"Certainly, sir."

"I should say, then, that this peculiarly constructed monster is the result of human hands and ingenuity."

"In that case, it is not a monster at all."

"By no means; I am very much in the dark at present, but I am positive that there is some wonderful mystery about this thing, which to my mind is a sort of submarine ship, ingeniously constructed to sail under the water for a time, and to come to the surface for a supply of fresh air from time to time. In short; an electric submarine boat."

CHAPTER XII

INSIDE OF THE "SEARCHER"

All three of the boys were greatly astonished.

"It beats the Dutch!" cried Carl.

"If that is so," said Mont, "there must be some internal mechanism to make it work about."

"Evidently."

"It gives no sign of life."

"Not at present," answered the man of science. "But we have seen it move. It has appeared and disappeared. Consequently, it must have hidden machinery."

"Of course."

"So that we come to the conclusion, which is inevitable, that there must be a man or men inside to direct the ship."

"Hurrah!" cried our hero; "I didn't think of that. We are saved if that is so, and it must be as you say."

"Hum!" muttered the professor; "I don't know so much about that. If, when it makes a start, it glides along the surface of the water, we are all right; but if it goes down, we are lost."

"I've got an idea," said Mont, after a pause. "We must knock at the door, and see if we can find anyone at home."

His companions laughed.

"I have searched carefully," said Carl, "but I can't find even a manhole."

There was nothing to do but to wait until morning.

Mont wanted to keep his feet warm, so he amused himself by kicking his heels upon the body beneath him.

"I'll wake 'em up," he said. "They shan't sleep if they won't let me in."

Their safety depended absolutely upon the caprice of the mysterious steersman who inhabited the ironclad, fish-shaped machine.

It seemed to the professor that before those inside descended again they would have to open some hole to obtain air.

All were now very tired, wet, and hungry, and soon a raging thirst began to attack them.

Our hero fancied he heard vague sounds beneath him, but could not be sure.

Who were the strange beings that lived in the floating iron shell?

Kicking angrily upon the iron surface, Mont said:

"You are very inhospitable inside. I am hungry and thirsty. Do you want me to die up here?"

He had no sooner spoken than a flap beside him opened and a railing came up as if by magic.

Half the body of a strong, wiry, thick-bearded man appeared. He held a curious wire net.

The net fell over Mont's head, and he felt himself dragged over the railing and down into the interior of the iron shell.

A cry of terror broke from his companions, answered by a smothered yell from Mont, as the flap fell back and shut out any further view of the interior.

Our hero had vanished.

This removal, so brutally executed, was accomplished with the rapidity of lightning.

Dr. Woddle felt his hair stand on end, and as for Carl and Stump they were chilled to the marrow of their bones with fear.

"What have they done with him?" Carl asked.

"Your friend is the first victim," replied the professor. "Perhaps they mean to eat him. For my part, they may eat me as soon as they like; anything is preferable to this."

"I wish I could get at them," replied Stump. "I'd soon have Master Mont out."

The words were scarcely out of his mouth when the trap door opened again, and the servant was dragged down below in a similar manner.

"Really this is very extraordinary," said the professor; "two of us are gone. We are no doubt in the hands of pirates, wretched rovers of the sea, who have brought science to their aid. It is to be hoped—"

The door opened while he was speaking and a long arm twining round his waist dragged him too into the heart of this floating prison.

His legs kicking up ludicrously in the air attracted the attention of Carl, who could not refrain from laughing, miserable though he was.

"My turn next," muttered the youth.

He was not long kept in suspense.

The long net twined, snakelike, round him, and he too descended into the bowels of the infernal machine.

Mont's experience was that of all of them.

He had descended an iron ladder and was pushed into a room, the door of which shut to with a heavy bang.

In ten minutes they were all together in the same compartment.

The darkness of their prison was so intense as to prevent our hero seeing his hand before his face.

Thus it was impossible to guess where they were, or even to

tell if they were alone or not.

"This is an outrage," said the doctor. "I protest against it. Is the author of a dozen immortal works to be treated like a naughty schoolboy?"

"We're prisoners," remarked Mont, "and it's no use hallooing. They're not going to eat us. This isn't an oven, and I think we are better here than up above."

"At least we had our liberty," continued the doctor, who was never satisfied or happy unless he was at work or grumbling.

"I've got a knife," said Stump boldly, "and I'll stick the first that comes near me. It's a regular pig-sticker, my knife, and I'll bet they feel it."

"Don't you do anything of the sort!" cried Mont. "You might get us all killed."

"It's very hard if a poor boy can't do something."

"You'll get it hot if anyone is listening to you. If you don't care for yourself, think of us."

Stump grumbled inaudibly, and Mont began to take the dimensions of the prison in which they were.

This he did by walking about, and he made it twenty feet long by ten wide. The walls were of iron, made of plates riveted together.

Half an hour passed. At the expiration of that time, the cabin was illuminated by a flood of light so vivid and blinding that it was difficult to bear the intensity.

Mont recognized the electric light that had floated round the ship when he first saw it.

When he got used to its clear whiteness, he looked up and saw that it proceeded from a globe which hung from the ceiling.

"Light at last; our captors are becoming more civil," said the doctor, rubbing his hands gayly.

"It's about time, I think," answered our hero.

They were not much better off, however, for the cabin only contained a table and five wooden stools, but the light was refreshing and made them more cheerful.

Not a sound reached their ears; everywhere reigned the silence of the grave.

Perhaps the ship had sunk to the bottom of the ocean, for it seemed to have the power of going where its strange owner wished.

In a short time the door opened and two men appeared.

"Visitors at last!" murmured Mont to himself.

CHAPTER XIII

THE OWNER OF THE SUBMARINE MONSTER

Of the two who had entered one was a negro, with intelligent but flat face, and short, woolly hair.

The other was a tall, handsome white man, with keen, searching eyes that looked into the very soul.

He wore a thick mustache, whiskers, and beard, and appeared to be an American.

He regarded the prisoners with a fixed gaze and said something to the negro in an unknown language, which was so sweet and soft that it seemed to be all vowels and no consonants.

At length he fixed his eyes upon the doctor, who, as the eldest of the party, seemed to be the leader of it. The professor made a low bow.

"I presume," he said, "that I am in the presence of the proprietor of this singular machine, and as I am a man of science I respect one who could conceive and carry out the idea of a submarine ship."

There was no answer.

"Permit me to tell you our history," continued the professor.

Still no reply.

"He's remarkably polite," remarked Mont. "Perhaps he don't understand our language."

"Leave him to me," said the professor; "my name may have an effect upon him. I am Dr. Homer Woddle, Professor of Natural History, and Secretary to the Society for the Exploration of the Unknown Parts of the World. I have written valuable books, sir, which have been translated into foreign languages."

The professor paused to look proudly around him.

Nothing in the face of the man before them indicated that he understood one word.

Undaunted by this silence, the doctor continued:

"This, sir, is my friend Mr. Mont Folsom, this my friend Mr. Carl Barnaby. The lad is their servant."

There was still no answer, and then the professor grew cross.

He spoke in French, then in German, finally in Greek and Latin; but with the same disheartening effect.

Not a muscle of the stranger's face moved.

Turning to the right, he muttered some words in his incomprehensible language, and, without making any reassuring sign to the prisoners, turned on his heel and walked away, the door closing after him.

"Well, I'm blowed!" said Mont. "This is a queer go, and no mistake."

"I know one thing," said Carl; "that is, I am dying with hunger."

"If they would only give me a saucepan and some fire," said Stump, "I'd make some soup."

"How?"

"I've got my boots, and the Unknown who came in let his sealskin cap fall. I picked it up and sneaked it. The two together wouldn't make bad soup."

While he spoke the door opened again, and another negro entered with a tray upon which were four plates.

A savory smell issued from them. Knives and forks were provided, and having placed the plates on the table the negro raised the covers.

"Food!" said Mont; "that's good."

"Not up to much, Master Mont, I'll bet," observed Stump.

"What do you know about it?"

"What can they give us? Porpoise stew, fillets of dogfish, or stewed shark. I'd rather have some salt junk on board the ship."

The negro disappeared with the covers, and all but Stump sat down.

"Fire away, Stump," said Mont, looking at the dishes.

"After you; I can wait," replied the boy-of-all-work.

"Sit down, I tell you. When people are shipwrecked they are all equal. Pitch in," answered Mont.

Stump sat down. There was no bread, tea, or coffee, but a bottle of water supplied its place.

It was difficult to say what the dinner consisted of. It was a mixture of fish and vegetable matter, but not an atom of meat.

For some time no one spoke. The business of eating was all-absorbing, for one must eat, especially after a shipwreck.

It was consoling to reflect they were not destined to die of hunger.

"I think," exclaimed Stump, when he had finished his plate, "that they mean to fatten us before they kill us!"

"Hold your tongue till you are spoken to," said Mont.

"Yes, sir. I know I'm only an odd boy, but—"

"Shut up, I tell you. I want to go to sleep."

"Certainly, sir. Sorry I took the liberty, but if I don't talk to somebody I must talk to myself."

"Try it on, that's all, and if you wake me when I'm asleep, I'll give you something for yourself. I'm just getting dry, and shall sleep like a top," answered our hero, throwing himself in a corner.

The professor, who was worn out, had already chosen his corner.

Carl followed his example, and soon all slept.

CHAPTER XIV

THE ATTACK

How long he slept Mont did not know.

He woke first, and saw his companions snoring like those who are over-tired.

Nothing was changed in the apartment, except that the remains of the dinner had been removed.

It was with difficulty that he managed to breathe, and he guessed that he had consumed all the oxygen in his prison. His lungs were oppressed, and the heavy air was not sufficient for proper respiration.

While Mont was arranging his toilet a valve opened in the side of the room, and a fresh current of sea air swept into the cabin.

Evidently the vessel had ascended to the surface of the ocean and taken in a fresh supply of air.

The others, influenced by this invigorating atmosphere, woke up, and rubbing their eyes started to their feet.

Stump looked at Mont and asked if he had slept well.

"Pretty well. How are you, Mr. Professor?"

"I breathe the sea air, and I am content," answered Dr. Woddle. "How long have we slept? It must be four-and-twenty hours, at least, for I am hungry again; I cannot tell to a certainty, for my watch has stopped."

"There is one comfort," replied Mont, "we are not in the hands of cannibals, and we shall be well treated."

"I don't know about that," said Stump. "They've got no fresh meat on board; all they gave us yesterday was fishy stuff; and four fine, fat, healthy fellows—"

"Shut up, Stump," cried Mont; "how often am I to tell you to hold your tongue?"

"I know I'm only an odd boy, but—"

"Will you be quiet?" exclaimed our hero, taking up a stool threateningly.

"All right; I won't say anything more."

The doctor was very silent and thoughtful. Mont remarked this, and said:

"How long do you think they will keep us here?"

"I can't tell any more than you, Folsom," replied the professor.

"But what is your opinion?"

"Not a very encouraging one. We have by chance become

possessed of an important secret. If the secret is worth more than our lives, we shall either be killed or kept prisoners."

"Forever?"

"Yes, forever," answered the professor gravely. "If the secret is not very serious, we may be landed on some island. I advise that we remain perfectly quiet and take things as they come."

"May I say a word?" exclaimed Stump.

"Well?" asked Mont.

"I'll get out of this."

"How? It is difficult to break out of a prison on earth, but to get out of one under the sea is impossible."

"Suppose we kill our jailers and take the key? If four Americans aren't a match for a lot of niggers, and one Unknown who can't speak any language, and doesn't belong to any country at all, it's time we shut up shop!" went on Stump.

At that moment the door opened, and the negro who had before appeared entered.

Stump instantly threw himself upon him, and, seizing his throat with his two hands, held him so tightly as almost to strangle him.

But being a powerful man, he soon disengaged himself, and a fearful struggle ensued between them.

"Help, help!" cried the negro, in excellent English.

Stump let go his hold at this, and fell back laughing.

"So you can talk English!" he cried; "that's all right. I only flew at you to see what countryman you were. Now, then, tell us all about this ship, or I'll give you another dose."

Putting his finger to his lips, the negro gave a peculiar whistle—prolonged and shrill.

This was evidently a signal, for he had scarcely finished when the Unknown appeared on the threshold.

He was followed by six powerful negroes, all armed to the teeth.

It looked as if Mont and his friends were to be executed on the spot.

Roy Rockwood

CHAPTER XV

PRISONERS

For several minutes the master of the submarine monster gazed in silence at those in the iron-bound cabin.

Stump stood shivering in a corner.

"Please don't kill us!" he cried. "I—I—didn't mean any harm."

The strange owner of the still stranger craft looked at Stump for a moment, and then smiled faintly.

"Depart!" he cried to the negroes, and on the instant every one of the heavily armed men vanished.

Sitting down on the edge of the table, with his arms crossed on his powerful chest, this strange being seemed plunged in deep thought.

Our heroes regarded him with expectation, not unmixed with awe, for they were entirely in his power.

Was he about to punish them for the indiscretion of one of their number?

At length he spoke in English.

"Gentlemen," he said, "you see I can speak your language. I did not answer you at first, because I was undecided what to do with you. I am well acquainted with the scientific works written by Dr. Woddle, and I esteem it an honor to have made his acquaintance."

The professor bowed his acknowledgment of this compliment.

"I am also glad to see two intelligent young gentlemen like Mr. Folsom and Mr. Barnaby."

"You've forgotten me, sir," said Stump. "I'm only an odd boy, but—"

The captain extended his arm, and the hired boy was silent.

"I'm a man," he continued, "who has broken with society and renounced the world. Had you not molested me and fired at my vessel, I should not have crippled your ship and upset your boat. The attack came from your side."

"But, sir," answered the professor, "we took your ship to be some unknown creature."

"Possibly, but this creature had done you no harm. I saw you all take refuge outside, and I hesitated a long while what to do with you. I knew nothing of you. What were you to me? Why should I extend my hospitality to you? All that was necessary to break off your connection, was to give a signal to my engineers, and the *Searcher*, which is the name of my vessel, would have sunk to the bottom of the ocean. I had the right to do it."

Roy Rockwood

His hearers shuddered at this avowal.

"It seems to me that we are to be prisoners?" observed the professor.

"Certainly."

"But this is an outrage!" exclaimed Mont. "I demand to be put on shore at the nearest port, or given up to the nearest ship we meet."

"You will none of you ever see the earth again, or set foot upon it," replied the captain with much emphasis.

"This floating prison is, then, our tomb—our coffin, in which we must live and die?"

"Call it what you will," replied the captain. "You have obtained the secret of my existence. Do you think I could ever allow you to revisit the world, to let it be known through every newspaper how I pass my life?"

"How are we to address you, sir?"

"My name is Vindex. By my men I am called the Wizard of the Sea."

"Very well, Captain Vindex of the *Searcher*," said Mont, "we must make the best of our situation, but I will never give my word that I will not attempt to escape."

"I like you, boy, for your honesty," said the Wizard of the Sea, "though I warn you that if you are caught in the attempt, you will be instantly put to death."

"To death? You dare not!"

The captain laughed in a wild, weird manner.

"Dare not!" he said. "Foolish lad, there are no laws for me. I am the sole master here. My black slaves only live to do my bidding. What is your life or death to me? I have no more to say at present. Follow this negro into another cabin, where a repast awaits you."

He called to someone outside, and, bowing politely, went away, while the four companions were conducted to a dining room handsomely furnished and lighted by an electric lamp.

Various preparations invited their attention. The dinner service was of silver, and everything denoted immense wealth on the part of the owner.

The negro waited upon them attentively.

"What's your name?" asked Mont.

"Me name One, massa."

"One!"

"Yes, massa. There twelve slaves on board this ship, and all have figure names, me One, other nigger Two, other Three, Four, Five, Six, Seven, Eight, and so on up to Twelve."

"That's a queer idea," said our hero; "fancy calling out for your servant, and saying, 'Here, Nine, I want you,' or 'I say, Three, do this'!"

"It is my opinion," exclaimed the professor, "that Captain Vindex is a very remarkable man—the most remarkable, in fact, that ever lived. He has invented a singular ship which can go under the sea at will, but why not? Was not the

Roy Rockwood

invention of steam engines laughed at, as well as the invention of gas? Who, a hundred years ago, would have believed in the electric telegraph, by means of which we send a message to the end of the earth in a minute?"

"Very true," replied Mont. "And don't forget the telephone, and the submarine boat the government is trying to build. It's a pity a man of such genius should shut himself up like this, though."

"It is a pity," answered the professor.

"What's worse, though," remarked Carl, "is that he means to keep us as prisoners."

"If he can," said Stump.

"Don't you be so fast, Stump, my boy," said Mont. "Keep your mouth shut, or you may get into trouble."

"Very sorry, but I don't like such goings-on, and wish I was back again on the shore."

The negro handed the professor a fresh dish.

"Will massa have some oysters stewed in whale's milk?" he asked; "or some jam made of sea anemones?"

"I'd rather you'd not tell me what the dishes are; it will set me against them if you do," answered the professor with a wry face.

When the repast was ended, Mont jumped up. "I feel better," he said. "Mister Number One."

"Massa call me?" asked the black, who was clearing away.

"Yes. Where are we now?"

"We gone down, massa, and now we lie at the bottom of the sea."

Mont regarded him with undisguised astonishment.

The *Searcher* was indeed a wonderful craft.

CHAPTER XVI

THE MYSTERIES OF THE "SEARCHER"

Many days passed.

The lives of the captives were unvaried by any incident. They saw nothing of Captain Vindex; were well attended to, slept comfortably, and had nothing to complain of but their imprisonment.

Books were freely supplied them, but they were not allowed to leave their cabins.

At the expiration of a fortnight or thereabouts, as well as they could reckon, negro Number One entered their cabin after breakfast.

Addressing Mont, the negro observed:

"Massa Folsom to come to cappen's cabin."

"Does he want me?" inquired Mont. "All right. Good-by, my friends," he added, "perhaps you will never see me again. I may be the first victim."

"No fear!" exclaimed Carl. "We shan't be hurt if we

keep quiet."

"I'll suggest that you're the fattest, Carl, if there is any question of cooking one of us."

"Then it won't be true, for you're as fat as a mole. Go on and be cooked first! I'll have a bit of you," answered Barnaby.

Mont went away laughing. He was not really alarmed, for although he did not like Captain Vindex, he fancied he was safe as long as he did not irritate this strange being.

The negro conducted him along a passage which opened into a magnificent library, full of books, which gave admittance to a drawing room furnished with all the taste that could be found in Paris or New York.

The space within the ironclad shell had been made the most of, and no expense had been spared to make the cabin luxurious and well appointed.

The walls were richly papered and covered with valuable paintings. The ceiling was frescoed, and works of art were everywhere to be seen. Rich couches and chairs invited rest, and the foot sank in the soft pile of a Turkey carpet.

Captain Vindex arose as our hero entered.

"Take a seat," he said, as the negro retired, closing the door after him. "I have taken an interest in you, Folsom."

"Thank you," answered Mont coldly.

The captain smiled, approached the end of the room, and, drawing back a curtain, revealed a splendid organ.

"Do you like music?" he asked.

"Very much," answered Mont. "Play us something. It will enliven me a bit. I feel awfully low, and I'll give you a game at dominoes or checkers afterwards, if you like."

Captain Vindex smiled, and, sitting down, played Sousa's "Liberty Bell March" with great skill.

"Thank you," said Mont, when he had finished. "Very fine. Now will you tell me how you manage for air?"

"I will not trouble you with chemical details," answered the captain, "which you would not understand, but when I do not take in air at the surface, I have some compressed in the reservoir, which, by means of an apparatus, is wafted all over the ship."

"And about light and moving about?"

"That is the result of electricity, which I make myself. My motive power is electricity, and I can attain a speed of thirty miles an hour. The men of the world have not yet discovered half the value of electricity. My machinery is of the finest kind. If I want to sink to the bottom of the sea, I fill certain reservoirs I have with water; when I want to rise, I lighten the ship by letting out the water. In short, I have invented everything that is necessary for my safety and comfort."

"Wonderful!" ejaculated Mont.

"Your friend, the professor, would understand me, if I were to explain to him how everything were managed, but to you it all seems as strange as the first railway train did to the country people through whose districts it passed. Enginee-ring science is yet in its infancy. The world has great discoveries to make. You are at present only on the threshold of the great unknown."

"You work your ship with a screw, I suppose?"

"Exactly. The helmsman sits in a cabin with a glass front, and the electric light illumines the sea for some distance, so that all is clear to him."

"Where did you build this extraordinary vessel?" continued our hero.

"On a desert island in the Pacific. I had the various parts brought in a vessel that belonged to me from various parts of the world, and the twelve negroes who are now with me were my only workmen."

"You are rich, then?"

"Money was never any object to me," replied the captain. "If I wanted gold even now, could I not obtain millions from the bottom of the sea out of ships that have sunk? And some day I shall find the great million-dollar pearl for which I am searching. The treasures of the deep are mine; I am the Wizard of the Sea."

He spoke proudly, and his eyes dilated with rapture.

"You like the sea?"

"I love it. I revel in it. Look at the solitude and freedom I enjoy! What life can be comparable to mine?"

"But you must feel weary at times," said Mont.

"Never. I read, I think, and, when I want diversion, I shoot."

"Where?"

"In the submarine forests. I have invented a square case to strap on the back, which is attached to a mask covering the head, and this will contain enough compressed air to last for several hours' consumption, so that I can walk under the waves with ease and comfort."

"And your guns?"

"Are air guns, also my own invention. I have several, and each is prepared to fire twenty shots by a mere movement of the trigger, the requisite force of air being placed in a hollow of the butt end; but all these mysteries will become plain to you before you have been long with me," answered Captain Vindex.

"What time is it?" asked Mont.

Looking at his watch, the captain answered:

"A quarter to twelve, or near midday."

"If you want to give me a treat," said Mont, "I wish you would go up to the surface and let me have a look at the sea, and breathe the fresh air."

"Certainly. Come with me to the engine room."

Mont rose, and followed his conductor through several iron passages to the place where the machinery was fitted up.

A negro saluted the captain.

"Number Twelve," exclaimed the latter, "I wish to ascend."

The engineer touched a valve, and a rush of water escaping was heard.

The pumps were forcing out the water from the reservoirs.

The *Searcher* began to ascend. After a time she stopped suddenly.

"We have arrived," said the captain.

He led the way up a central spiral staircase, and, raising a small door, they emerged upon what may be called the deck, or what our hero and his companions had taken to be the back of the monster.

Touching a spring, an iron railing sprang up, about five feet high.

This prevented any danger of falling into the sea in rough weather, for it made a small inclosure about twenty feet by ten.

Mont saw that the shape of the ship was something like a long cigar.

The sea was calm and the sky clear; a light breeze fanned their cheeks as Mont opened his lungs to take in the inviting atmosphere.

There was, however, nothing to be seen. All was one vast desert.

The captain proceeded, armed with a sextant, to take the height of the sun, which would give him his latitude.

He waited some minutes until the sun attained the edge of

the horizon.

Having calculated the longitude chronometrically, he said:

"To-day I commence a voyage of exploration under the waves."

"When you like," replied Mont; "anything for a little excitement."

The captain conducted him downstairs again, the iron railing fell, the trapdoor closed overhead, and with a bow the strange being left him to join his companions.

CHAPTER XVII

THE DEVIL FISH

"He's about half crazy!"

Such was Mont's conclusion as he joined his companions.

While Mont was telling the others of what he had seen, all were treated to a surprise.

A panel in the wall slid back.

A large sheet of very thick plate glass, quite transparent, was revealed to view almost immediately; a flood of electric light lit up the sea for some distance, and everything was as clear as daylight.

It was as if they were looking at an immense aquarium.

"The captain is giving us a surprise," remarked the professor; "this is charming."

Innumerable fishes of various kinds, most of which were unknown, even to a naturalist of Dr. Woddle's standing, passed before them.

Roy Rockwood

Strange, wild, fierce-looking things, with wonderful tails and heads.

Some looking unmistakably voracious, others being long and slimy like hideous snakes.

They were doubtless attracted by the electric light.

For two hours the four companions gazed at the ever-changing procession, without the least abatement of their delight.

Presently the door opened, and a negro handed the professor a letter.

He opened it and read its contents aloud.

"Captain Vindex presents his compliments to Professor Woddle, and will be glad if he and his companions will accept an invitation to shoot in the weed forests under the sea to-morrow morning at ten o'clock."

"I'll be hanged if I go!" exclaimed Stump. "Not if I know it. I'm safe here, but I don't want to be chawed up by some strange reptile."

"Silence, boy!" said the professor. "Tell Captain Vindex," he continued, to the negro, "that we are much obliged to him for his invitation, which we gladly accept."

The negro bowed and retired.

At the time appointed the professor and the boys were conducted to a cabin, which may be called the dressing-room, or arsenal, of the *Searcher*.

Hanging on the walls were numerous helmets, such as divers wear, and a number of guns reposed on hooks.

At the last moment Stump had determined to accompany the party.

Captain Vindex was already there, and received them graciously.

"I wish you good-day, professor," he said; "and you, too, my boys. I think we shall enjoy some excellent sport among the sea otters and other animals worth killing. You, Dr. Woddle, will be able to add to your knowledge of natural history, for we are about to traverse a forest of remarkable seaweeds and plants, in which you will find all kinds of submarine life."

"I am obliged to you for your kindness, sir, and put myself entirely at your disposal," replied the professor.

At a signal from the captain, two negroes assisted our heroes to put on their apparel, and clothed them in thick waterproof made of India rubber, which formed trousers and vest, the trousers terminating in a pair of shoes with lead soles; a cuirass of leather protected the chest from the pressure of the water, and allowed the lungs full play.

Supple gloves covered the hands, the helmet was then put on, and the knapsack of compressed air adjusted on the back.

To each one was given a gun, the butt of which was of brass and hollow.

Here was stored the compressed air which discharged the electric bullets, one of which fell into its proper place just as the other had been shot away. The whole mechanism was perfect.

When all was ready they stepped into an empty cabin, the door closed behind them, and, touching a knob, the captain allowed the room to fill with water.

Then he opened a door and they walked out into the sea.

Each had an electric lamp fastened to the waist, which made their path clear and distinct, enabling them to see every object through the glass holes in their helmets.

The captain walked in front with the professor.

Carl and Mont were side by side, and Stump brought up the rear.

Walking was not very difficult, and the supply of air, well charged with the oxygen necessary for prolonged respiration, was all that could be wished. It entered as it was required from the knapsack reservoir, and escaped when used through a turret at the top of the circular helmet.

They proceeded along fine sand, covered with a variety of shells, for at least a mile, when they came to some rocks covered with beautiful anemones.

Innumerable fish sported around them; long, writhing eels, of a prodigious size, with ugly, flat snake-like heads, glided away at their approach, and thousands of jelly fish danced about their heads.

They were not at a great depth, and presumably were near some island, for Mont, looking up, saw the sun overhead, guessing the depth to be about thirty or forty feet.

The sun's rays easily penetrated the waves, and made a kaleidoscope of colors inconceivably beautiful.

If the party could have spoken they would have given vent to their admiration in no measured terms.

The least sound was transmitted easily, showing that the sea is a better conductor of noise than land.

By degrees the depth increased, and they must have been a hundred yards from the surface, as the pressure of the water increased.

Mont suffered no inconvenience except a slight tingling in the ears and fingers.

He moved with ease, and was intensely delighted with the wonderful bed of sea flowers which gave place to the fine sand they had been traversing.

A dark mass extended itself before them; and Captain Vindex, extending his hand, indicated the beginning of the forest.

It was composed of large seaweeds and plants, which extended in a straight manner, having no drooping branches; all were erect and motionless.

When displaced by the hand they resumed a perpendicular position.

They scarcely had any roots in the sand, and were evidently nourished by the water and not by the earth.

Some were long and slender, others short and bushy, covered with blossoms of various colors; others, again, reached a height equal to our forest trees.

They had not proceeded far through this dense jungle of

weeds, among which it was difficult to pick a path, when the captain halted.

In front of him was a huge octopus, or devil fish, over three feet in diameter, with long, terrible arms.

It endeavored to seize the professor, who, sinking on his knees, shivered in silent terror!

CHAPTER XVIII

MONT IS LOST

It looked as if Professor Woddle's last moment had come.

In a moment more the devil fish had the shivering man in its fearful embrace.

The captain and Mont, however, raised their guns, and with one shot left it convulsed in its dying agonies.

As they continued to descend into a valley, bounded on each side by high rocks, the darkness increased, for the sun's rays could not penetrate more than a hundred and fifty yards.

It was now that the electric lamps became of importance.

As they got lower and lower, Mont felt an oppression about the head, and a great desire to sleep overcame him.

He lagged behind the others, and with difficulty kept up with them.

Several fine sea otters were seen in front, playing about amongst the weeds.

Roy Rockwood

The captain fired, and the others followed his example.

Three fell dead, one of which Stump took up and threw over his shoulder.

Suddenly Mont sank down on the ground and immediately fell asleep.

His companions, in the eagerness of their chase after the game that had escaped, did not notice his absence.

They had proceeded fully half a mile, when Barnaby, looking back, was unable to discover any trace of Mont.

He at once ran to the captain and made signs, pointing to himself, the professor, and Stump, and pointing in different directions to intimate that Mont was lost.

Captain Vindex at once comprehended his meaning.

He retraced his steps, going carefully over the ground they had trodden.

It was without success, for nowhere could they find the slightest trace of their unfortunate companion.

Carl would have given worlds had he been able to speak.

He was profoundly agitated, for it was horrible to think that his chum was lost under the sea, not knowing his way back to the *Searcher*, for they had come a roundabout way.

Captain Vindex was also annoyed.

If Mont chose he could climb up the rocks and reach the summit.

There he might take off his helmet, and breathe the free air of heaven.

But would he think of this?

Perhaps in his confusion he would wander about in the effort to meet his companions, and at last be suffocated miserably.

The supply of air with which each was provided was not sufficient to last more than five hours.

Two of those hours' supply had been already consumed.

It was necessary that Captain Vindex and those with him should think of returning to the ship.

Making a sign, he led the way back.

Carl felt inclined to stay and die in the attempt to find his friend.

It would have been an immense relief to him to have said something, but not a sound could he make audible outside his helmet.

With sad and weary steps they traversed the lovely valley, which had lost all its former attractions for the party.

The forest was passed and the sand regained.

They were not more than two miles from the *Searcher*.

Carl determined to make a last effort.

He seized the captain's arm and pointed pathetically, almost imploringly, to the dense mass of vegetation behind them.

His mute appeal to go back after Mont was comprehended.

But it was disregarded.

Their own lives would have been in jeopardy had they turned back.

The air in the reservoirs was becoming weak and impure.

Shaking his head in a negative manner, the captain pursued his way.

With a heavy heart Carl followed him, and in time the ship was reached.

They entered the water room, closed the doors, and the captain touched a bell.

Directly it sounded within the vessel, the pumps were heard at work, the water gradually lowered, and when it was all out they opened the inner door and regained the dressing-room.

It was indeed a pleasure to have the helmets removed, for they had retained them so long that they were oppressed and ill.

The captain was the first to speak.

"I am very sorry for the misfortune that has happened," he exclaimed; "you must not think me hard-hearted because I returned."

"But Mont will die," answered Carl; "he is lost, and does not know his way back."

"His supply of air will last another hour and a half. There is yet hope."

"What can we do?"

"I will send out a party to search for him, and I will head it myself," replied Captain Vindex.

At this generous offer Carl's heart was filled with fresh hope.

The captain gave orders for three negroes to accompany him.

They were soon dressed and supplied with air, Captain Vindex himself taking a fresh reservoir.

Then the ceremony of going out was repeated, and, as the exploring party quitted the ship, all Carl could do was to pray fervently for their success.

He, the professor, and Stump were very languid, and, in spite of their anxiety, they could not shake off the somnolent effects of their long walk.

Each sank down on the floor of their cabin, and was soon fast asleep.

How long they remained there they did not know.

Barnaby awoke, feeling a hand laid on his shoulder. It was Captain Vindex.

Springing to his feet in an instant, he said:

"Have you found him? Where is Mont?"

"Unhappily," said the captain, "we could find no trace of him."

"Why did I let him go last? I ought to have had him in front of me," cried Carl angrily. "Poor Mont! he is lying at the bottom of the sea, and I shall never see him again. Never, never!"

He covered his face with his hands, and the tears trickled down his cheeks.

"I have dispatched another party to seek for him," exclaimed the captain; "I am too worn out to go with them this time. If they find the body, we may restore him to consciousness."

"There is no hope," said Carl sadly; "you are the cause of his death. Why did you inclose us in this tomb, and then take one of us in the sea to die?"

"Was it my fault? You are hasty, my boy, and do me great injustice. I am as much grieved as yourself, for I had begun to love that lad," said the captain feelingly. "We will mourn for him together; there is a silent friendship in grief. We are friends, for we have the same sorrow."

In a few hours the searching party came back, weary and unsuccessful.

They could see nothing of Mont.

Everyone gave up all hope, and our hero was mourned for as one dead.

CHAPTER XIX

MONT'S PERIL

"Where am I? Where are you, Carl?"

After about an hour's sleep Mont was aroused by an acute sensation of pain in his right leg.

Stretching out his hand, he encountered a slimy substance, and withdrew it very quickly.

Leaning on his elbow, he saw by the light of his lamp that a strange fish, with a head like a frying-pan and a body resembling that of a codfish, was biting through his waterproof covering and trying to eat part of his leg.

In an instant he seized his gun, and, firing at its eye, wounded it grievously, causing it to splash about and retreat into a mass of weeds, where its struggles continued for some time.

For a moment Mont forgot where he was.

But as his senses came back to him, he recollected everything, and, rising, looked about for his companions.

As he could see nothing of them, a horrible fear took possession of him, and he trembled from head to foot.

They had lost him in the depths of the ocean.

Without an experienced guide like Captain Vindex, it was impossible for him to find his way back.

The dangerous and perhaps fatal sleep which had overcome him must be fought against.

For if it came on again he knew he must die.

How much precious air had he not consumed already?

To him, in his condition, air was life.

He knew that he had only a supply for a limited period.

The only course that remained open to him was to march as quickly as the dense mass of water would let him, and try to regain the *Searcher*.

But though he turned round, he could not find the sandy plain they had first traversed on leaving the ship.

The forest of sea weeds, rising straight as arrows on all sides of him, erect and motionless, grew dense; animal life was everywhere.

Strange fishes glared at him, and seemed to mock his misery by their quick, darting movements and sportive gambols.

He pushed his way fiercely through the vegetable growth, but only to become more entangled.

All at once the ground became hilly, and it seemed as if he had come to the end of the valley and was ascending one of the sides.

He pushed on, thinking he would give the world to be able to rise to the surface.

If he could only penetrate that thick water and float on the top of the waves, breathing the free air of heaven, he would have gladly done so, even if he were to die an hour afterward.

Gradually he quitted the forest, and the sun's rays began to be visible again.

Decidedly he must be getting higher.

Presently a great black mass appeared at his side.

He could see that it was a ferocious shark, whose huge mouth seemed capable of engulfing him.

Instinctively he threw himself on his back.

The voracious creature had made a dart at him, but shot past, disappointed of its prey.

If it had seized his arm or his leg, or even his head, one snap of its mouth would have been sufficient to cut off either.

As the animal swam around him Mont pointed his gun and fired.

The shot entered its stomach, but was not mortal.

Another and another followed, and at last the vast mass

floated slowly upward, showing that it was dead.

Thanking Providence for this narrow escape, and congratulating himself on his presence of mind, our hero continued the ascent.

The path became steep and rugged, and it was with difficulty that he made his way.

He was evidently ascending the side of a rock, which became more precipitous as he went on.

Where did it lead?

Was it raised above the surface or did it fall short of it?

If so, he would have his trouble for nothing.

He breathed with an effort, and his breath grew shorter and shorter every moment, for he was making a great demand upon his reservoir of air while undergoing strong exertion.

At length he had to stop.

It seemed as if his strength were failing him.

The sleepy feeling overtook him again, and he leaned back against the shining rock, which reflected the sun's rays.

He was face to face with death.

Not much longer would his lungs be supplied with breathing air.

Suffocation threatened Mont with a painful end, yet he was so weak and prostrate that he seemed unable to make another effort.

Every moment was of priceless value.

At last he went on.

How he did it he never knew; but he managed to climb the almost perpendicular rocks, which afforded little or no footing.

At last the sun's rays were more vivid, and, with a feeling of wonder, Mont found himself moving with comparative ease.

This was because he had reached the summit of the rock after climbing nearly two hundred and fifty yards.

He was out of the water.

With nervous hands he tore off his helmet, and, lying on his side, inhaled the air for a few minutes.

"I am saved, saved!" cried Mont delightedly.

He rose at length, and looked around him.

The rock on which he was standing was a narrow, barren peak, which just rose above the surface, and that was all.

The remainder of the ledge was under water. If he had not ascended in that place he must have died.

Afar off was what appeared to be a small island. But whether it was an arid desert or not he was unable to tell.

"Perhaps I shall die of hunger and thirst," he muttered; "but death is better here than in the forest under the sea."

Sleep again overcame him, and he passed several hours in a deep slumber.

With wakefulness came a horrible sensation of hunger and thirst.

While he was gazing around him, with despair again attacking him, he saw something rise in the sea a short distance off.

He thought he recognized the black back of the *Searcher*, and he was not mistaken.

The trapdoor opened, and two men appeared on the platform.

They were Captain Vindex and Professor Woddle.

Mont tried to cry out, but only a feeble sound came from his lips.

He, however, waved his hands, and the signal was seen.

Soon the electric boat floated gently to the rock.

He stepped on the platform, which was by this time crowded with the crew, Carl, and Stump.

The next moment he was in the arms of kind friends.

He sank fainting at their feet, and was carried below, where he remained some days before he entirely recovered his strength.

Captain Vindex had entertained an idea that Mont might reach the surface by climbing up the rocks, although he scarcely dared to hold this opinion as a certainty.

But when nothing could be seen of him below the surface, he resolved to look for him above.

Consequently the *Searcher* rose under his orders, with the happy result we have described.

Roy Rockwood

CHAPTER XX

THE WRECKS

When Mont was fully recovered, the negro Number One announced that they were going on a long voyage.

"Massa say him start for, um South Pole," he said. "In one hour we be off, and travel for many week. Travel to the Pole."

In effect, they soon heard the motion of the machinery, and the *Searcher* began her long submarine cruise.

For about a week they saw nothing of the captain.

This mysterious man shut himself up and sought intercourse with no one.

Every day, for some hours, the panel in their cabin slid back, and they enjoyed the treat of looking at the sea lighted by electricity.

The direction of the *Searcher* was southeast, and she kept at a depth of a hundred to a hundred and fifty feet.

One day, while the electric ship was stopping to replenish

her power, a curious incident happened.

Stump was looking out of the window, and he suddenly exclaimed:

"What is that, sir?"

Everyone went to examine, and a ship dismantled was seen slowly sinking to the bottom.

It had foundered a short time before with all hands.

Several men were lashed to the riggings, and their agonized faces testified to their late sufferings.

A shoal of sharks followed the sinking wreck with distended eyes, anticipating a feast of human flesh.

As the hull passed the window, Mont read her name, which was the *Firefly* of Savannah.

This was not an isolated case, for they frequently saw wrecks, and remains of wrecks, such as cannons, anchors, chains, and decaying hulls.

"Well, this is a lively existence," exclaimed Mont; "we eat nothing but fish, and see nothing but fish."

"And wrecks," put in Carl.

A heavy step was heard behind them, and all turned round, to see the captain.

He placed his hand upon a map, and exclaimed:

"Do you see this island—Malonon? It is where the gallant

French explorer Posterri perished. We are close to it, and, if you please, gentlemen, you shall land and explore it for yourselves."

This was good news.

"But," said the professor, "if I remember rightly, it is inhabited by savages."

"Certainly."

"Shall we not be in danger?"

"I fear nothing," said the captain. "I have braved danger among civilized nations, and I can afford to despise savages. If you do not wish it, however, I will continue my voyage."

"Don't do that, sir," replied Mont. "I'll chance the niggers. Let us land. I know Carl and Stump would like it."

"And you, Mr. Professor?" said the captain.

"I, sir, will go anywhere in the interests of science," replied Homer Woddle, with a nervous tremor in his voice which showed he did not like savages.

The news raised the boys' spirits to the highest pitch.

After confinement on board the *Searcher* the prospect of going on land was enchanting.

No matter what danger they might encounter they were ready.

Carl whispered that they might have a chance of escaping.

Mont said nothing, but he was of the same opinion.

CHAPTER XXI

ON LAND ONCE MORE

The party were allowed to go on shore without even promising to return, and the heart of each beat high with the prospect of liberty before them.

Professor Woddle explained that they might traverse the country nearby, and so get to some port, but the journey would be perilous in the extreme.

His advice was to camp in the wood, obtain fresh provisions, and await the course of events.

Stump alone was in doubt.

"The captain," he remarked, "is a wonderful man, and knows perfectly well what he is about. He has told us we shall never again set our feet on civilized ground, has he not?"

"Yes. Everyone knows that," answered the professor.

"He'll keep his word, and I'll bet a new hat we are on board again to-morrow, or perhaps to-day."

"I'll take you," replied Mont, "though how the bet is to be

paid I don't know, as there are no hat shops on board the boat."

"I'd give something to find out all about our skipper," said Carl. "He is the most curious beggar I ever met. All four of us are not a match for him."

"Speak for yourself, my young but still intelligent friend," answered the professor. "Time will show."

"We'll have some fresh meat soon," observed Stump, "and if you'll trust the cooking to me, Master Mont, you shall have a dinner fit for a king in half an hour after running down the game."

"A little venison or wild boar, which is pork, would be very acceptable," answered the professor; "and my knowledge of natural history enables me to tell you that we shall find both on this island which we are about to visit."

"Roast pork—lovely! It makes my mouth water," said Stump.

"Do you want to have the jaw all to yourself?" asked Mont. "Go and ask when the boat will be ready to take us ashore."

Stump departed on his errand and found the boat already prepared for them.

It was made of various pieces of wood, which were easily put together when it was wanted and taken apart when it was not required.

It would hold half a dozen men, and floated by the side of the *Searcher*.

Each of the four companions was provided with an electric gun containing the usual twenty shots.

"A pleasant excursion, gentlemen," said the captain, as they emerged on the platform; "I hope you do not intend to deprive me for any length of time of the pleasure of your society."

"Wouldn't do such a thing for worlds, sir," answered our hero.

"You needn't return to-night, if you prefer camping out."

"We didn't mean to," replied Mont.

A peculiar smile crossed Captain Vindex's expressive face, as if he guessed what was passing in the youth's mind.

"Remember one thing," he said; "be very careful of your ammunition."

"Why?"

"You will find out in time. All I have to say is, recollect my advice," was the answer.

They got into the boat and rowed ashore, picking their way carefully through the coral reefs, and in five minutes the bottom of the boat grated upon a sandy beach.

"Hurrah!" cried Mont, throwing up his cap; "land once more!"

Stump, who was thoroughly familiar with all the tricks of boys, put down his hands and "turned a wheel," after which he stood on his head, to give expression to his delight.

Huge forests stretched far inland, and raised their mighty heads a hundred feet from the earth.

Palms, shrubs, and creepers were mingled with the trees in grand confusion, and this scene, in the glowing sunshine, was indescribably beautiful.

The professor saw a cocoanut palm, and, knocking off some of the fruit, gave it to the boys, who pronounced it delicious.

"Now," he said, "we will shoot something and dine as we have not dined for a long time."

"I've some salt in my pocket, and Stump has knives," remarked Carl.

"It looks to me," said Mont, "as if we were likely to have a sirloin of tiger for dinner; that forest ought to be full of wild beasts."

"No matter," answered Carl, "anything's better than fish. Come on."

They skirted the forest, fearing to enter it lest they might lose themselves in its dense interior.

Keeping their guns ready for instant action, they proceeded about half a mile, when the professor held up his hand.

In front of them was a large breadfruit tree, and under its branches was a wild boar, engaged in eating the tender fruit which had fallen to the ground.

"Approach gently, and fire all together," said the professor.

They did so, and four shots were discharged at the

same time.

The wild boar uttered a ferocious grunt, ran a few paces, and fell down dead.

"What is it, sir?" asked Carl.

"A wild boar; do you not see his tusks? Now, Stumpton, set to work, and cut a leg of pork off piggy. You, Folsom, make a fire with the dry wood; it will kindle when I rub two sticks together. You, Barnaby, gather some of this fruit."

"Is it good to eat, sir?"

"You will find it excellent. I recognize it as the breadfruit of the tropics, and, cut up in slices and toasted over the fire, nothing could be better for us with our roast pork," answered the professor.

They were quickly at work. The fire was lighted, the leg of pork cut off and fixed to a tripod, the breadfruit toasted, and plates supplied by large palm leaves. Presently a delicious odor of roast pork spread itself around.

After living so long on the peculiar fare provided by Captain Vindex, they enjoyed their dinner immensely; and, when they had satisfied their appetites, they sat down under the shade of a tree, sheltered from the noontide heat.

"Now, sir," said Mont, "what are we to do?"

"I have no wish to return to our floating prison," replied the professor. "The question is, shall we go back, or shall we try to make our way to some port, risking the dangers of the way, the chances of starvation?"

"That does not appear likely," answered Mont, thinking of the roast pork and the breadfruit.

"When our guns are empty, we may not find it so easy to kill game, however abundant it may be. The savages are another danger."

"Put it to the vote, sir," said our hero.

"Certainly; all you who wish to make an effort to escape from the thralldom in which we are held, hold up your hands."

Every hand was extended.

"To the contrary?"

There was no response.

"Not a hand," said the professor. "I may, then, conclude, that we are unanimous in our wish for freedom, and it is decided that we do not return to the *Searcher*."

"Hurrah!" cried Stump, proceeding to stand on his head again.

"If you don't stop those street-arab tricks," remarked Mont, "you'll have a fit, after such a meal as you've had."

Stump resumed his natural position.

"There's no lie, sir, about my having had a filler of pork," he replied. "But though I'm only an odd boy, I've got my feelings, and I'd as soon be a convict as in that there prison ship."

"The youth is right," observed the professor mildly; "to live and die in that ship is an awful prospect, and I would rather herd with savages in their wilds than do it."

And as if it was intended as an answer to his speech, an arrow flew over his head.

Fortunately it missed its mark, and stuck quivering into the bark of the tree under which they were sitting.

Everyone sprang to his feet, and stood, gun in hand, on the defensive.

"Savages, by George!" exclaimed Mont.

"Where?" asked the professor.

"To the right, sir. Fire away, and chance it, or we shall all be killed."

There was an instant discharge of firearms, and a scuffling was heard behind some cactus and mimosa bushes.

A dozen savages, nearly naked, armed with spears and bows and arrows, were seen in a state of hesitation, whether to fly or stand their ground.

Three of their number had fallen from the discharge, and one, who was mortally wounded, was crawling, in a slow, labored manner, into the bush to die.

CHAPTER XXII

FIGHTING THE SAVAGES

"They are retreating!" cried Mont joyfully.

"No! no! they are coming on again!" put in Carl, a few seconds later.

"At 'em again, boys; let them have it," said the professor.

"Hot and strong this time, sir," said Stump, advancing a step to take better aim.

Again the bullets flew, and three more savages went down.

The others turned to fly to the shelter of the neighboring forests.

"Hurrah! they're bolting," said Mont.

"But they've collared what was left of our bread, and the remains of the roast pork," said the hired boy angrily. "Oh, the varmints! I'll just give them something."

He advanced to fire better.

An aged chief, however, turned at this moment and discharged a parting shot which took effect in the calf of Stump's leg.

"Oh, dear! I'm hit," he cried. "A great wooden skewer's stuck right in my leg, sir. Perhaps it's poisoned, sir. Oh, dear, but I wish it hadn't been me. There's the professor, now; he could have borne it better than me."

"Thank you, my young friend," said the professor, "the calf of my leg is as susceptible to pain as yours; let us get away, as arrowheads are sharp, and in certain parts of the body mortal."

"Where shall we go?" asked Mont.

"We are not safe here. The savages will return in larger numbers directly, and we shall probably lose our lives, so I propose to seek our boat."

"And go back to the *Searcher*?" asked Carl.

"Yes."

"Never! I for one will not go!" cried Carl.

"And I can't crawl. I'm as lame as a dog," said Stump, half crying.

"Roll, if you can't walk," said the professor jokingly.

"Pull it out, sir. Give me a hand with it. It hurts awful."

Mont advanced to the boy and seized the arrowhead, which he tugged at until, with a torrent of blood, it came out of the wound.

It was with difficulty Stump managed to limp on one leg, and seemed very grateful when Mont bound up the wound and told him to lean on his shoulder.

"My dear boy," said the professor, "discretion is the better part of valor. I am averse to the taking of human life, for I am a man of science and not a fighter. My advice is to check the advance of those bloodthirsty savages, and when your ammunition is spent, to run. As I am old, and not quick of foot, I will start at once."

So saying, he ran with all speed to the boat.

"Coward!" said Mont angrily.

"What are we to do?" asked Carl blankly.

"Follow him, I suppose," replied Mont. "Bring up the rear, Carl, while I help Stump along, and if the beasts show again, call us, and we will turn and fire."

They began to beat a retreat in this order, and, fortunately, the natives did not again make an appearance.

The half-mile was traversed quickly, Stump groaning dreadfully as he was forced along.

When within a few paces of the boat awful yells were heard behind them.

Turning to see from whence they proceeded, Mont saw a horde of savages in pursuit. The sands seemed to be alive with them.

Evidently the defeated party had returned to obtain re-enforcements and apprise their companions of the slaughter which had taken place, urging them to avenge it.

An army of at least three hundred wild-looking fiends were at their heels, and not a moment was to be lost.

"Quick, for Heaven's sake!" said Professor Woddle. "The savages are upon us. Quick, boys, or we are lost!"

The boys sprang into the boat, placing Stump in the bows, and pushed off.

Carl and Mont plied the oars vigorously.

Fortunately, when the savages reached the beach they were some distance out.

A flight of arrows fell close to them without doing them any harm.

At least a hundred of the natives plunged into the sea up to the waist, but they did not attempt to swim after the boat, which soon reached the *Searcher*.

Mont expected to see someone, but the platform was deserted.

Our hero at once went to the captain, being alarmed at the hostile attitude of the savages, whom he did not doubt were possessed of canoes and would make an attack upon the ship.

He was annoyed at being obliged to take shelter so soon, but what could he do?

All his hopes of liberty in flight were nipped in the bud.

He began to see now that Captain Vindex knew the character

of the coast, and had calculated well on their return to their captivity.

Imprisonment with him was better than death or slavery among the savages of the island.

The captain was sitting in front of the organ playing an exquisite air of Beethoven.

Full of excitement, Mont had no time to listen.

He touched him on the shoulder.

The Wizard of the Sea seemed unconscious of his presence.

"Captain," said our hero.

The strange being shivered and turned round.

"Ah," he cried, "'tis you, Mr. Folsom. Have you had good sport? You have returned sooner than I expected."

"The sport was not bad," replied Mont, "but unfortunately we met with a troop of savages, who spoilt our fun."

The captain smiled ironically.

"Savages!" he repeated. "Were you surprised at meeting with them? Have you so little geographical knowledge that you do not know they swarm hereabouts?"

"All I know is," replied Mont, "that if you don't want them on board the boat, you had better look out."

"My dear fellow," said the captain, "I am not likely to trouble my head about such wretches."

"But there are lots of them."

"How many?"

"Over three hundred, I should think, as well as I could count."

"We have nothing to fear from them, nothing at all," said the captain. "Don't be alarmed."

Without another word he turned again to the organ, and played a Scotch air which had an indescribable charm about it.

He was plunged again in a reverie that Mont did not think it prudent to interrupt.

He remounted to the platform without seeing a single negro.

The most absolute want of precaution reigned on board the *Searcher*, and it looked as if no one knew that hundreds of howling savages were within five minutes' row of them.

In the growing darkness, which came on while Mont was alone, he could see the forms of the natives running backward and forward on the beach.

They were evidently planning an attack upon a large scale.

What could account for the captain's strange apathy?

After a time he forgot the natives in admiring the lovely night of the tropics.

The zodiacal stars appeared, and the moon shone brightly amidst innumerable constellations of the zenith.

He wished that the moon would light the *Searcher* to the coral bed, and that they would sink to the bottom, where they would be safe from their enemies.

Proceeding below again he sought his friends.

The door giving access to the interior of the boat remained open, and he observed a slave standing at the bottom of the staircase as if on watch.

Stump had his leg plastered up, and, though in pain, was much better.

Strange to say, all were pleased to return to the boat, and to escape a fearful death of lifelong slavery among the savages, who are known to travelers as the Papouans.

Mont slept badly, for he anticipated a night attack.

CHAPTER XXIII

ELECTRIFYING THE SAVAGES

"What a sight! They are going to attack us, sure!"

It was Mont who spoke, as at six o'clock in the morning he ascended to the platform.

The morning mist had lifted, and he could see the land distinctly.

The savages were very busy, and more numerous than they had been the night before.

As well as he could calculate, he counted six or seven hundred of them.

They were tall, handsome men, with an erect bearing, their features well chiseled.

In their ears they wore rings of bone.

Their arms were bows and arrows, spears, and shields made of the skins of fish stretched over a wooden frame or the back of the turtle.

Roy Rockwood

A chief rowed in a canoe toward the *Searcher*, keeping at a safe distance.

He was adorned with a fantastic headdress of feathers and leaves, and seemed to be the king of the country.

Having nothing better to do, Mont got a fishing line from the negro who usually attended upon him, and amused himself with catching some of the fish that swam round the ship.

No one made any preparation to repel an attack of the Papouans, which alarmed Mont very much.

He had, however, so much confidence in the sagacity of Captain Vindex that he believed he would not be caught asleep.

For two hours he continued his sport with tolerable success, and was so wrapped up in it that he forgot the natives for the time.

While he was engaged in pulling up a good bite, an arrow whizzed past him.

Mont dropped his fish, and very nearly his line.

"Bother the brutes!" he exclaimed; "can't they let a fellow fish in peace? Why doesn't the captain make a start and get away from them?"

He was as eager now to leave the land as he had been the day before to reach it.

It was clear that the Papouans were puzzled.

They had seen European ships before, but what could they

make of a long cylinder of iron, without masts, almost flush with the surface of the water, and no chimney like a steamer?

But they gained confidence as they saw no attempt made to drive them away.

They had seen some of their number killed by the air-guns, yet they had heard no noise.

All at once a flotilla consisting of a score of canoes, full of savages, put off from the shore, and approached the ship.

Mont at once sought refuge in the interior of the ship, and ran to apprise the captain of the formidable state affairs were assuming.

Clearly no orders had been given to repel boarders.

Knocking at the captain's door, he was told to enter.

Captain Vindex was reading.

"Do I disturb you?" asked Mont politely.

"A little," replied the captain; "but I suppose you have good reason for seeking me?"

"Rather," answered our hero. "We are surrounded by savages, and in a few minutes we shall have them on board."

"Ah," said the captain, "they have got their canoes, I suppose?"

"Heaps of them."

"Then we must do something."

"Shut up the shop," said Mont.

"That is easily done," replied the captain, touching a bell, and adding: "In half a minute the trapdoor will be closed. You need not be afraid that they will break in."

"No, but to-morrow we shall want air, and you must open the door again for your pumps to work."

"Yes; our ship is like a great whale, and cannot live without air."

"In a moment the Papouans will be on the top of us, and I don't suppose they will go away in a hurry," replied Mont.

"You suppose they will take possession of the outside and keep it?"

"Exactly."

"Well, then," answered the captain calmly, "I don't see why they shouldn't. Why should I kill the poor creatures if I can help it? I know many savages in the civilized world whom I would cut off with more pleasure. Leave them to me. If it is necessary I will make a terrible example of them."

"You have no cannon."

"I shall not fire a shot, and I shall not wound them in any way, and yet they will fall like leaves in autumn. Go to your friends, and rest perfectly easy," said the captain.

This was a dismissal, and, wondering much, Mont went away.

As he sought his cabin he heard the fierce cries of the

savages, who swarmed on the back of the iron ship like flies in summer.

The night passed without any incident. Plenty of oxygen still passed through the ship, but it was time to renew the air, which was becoming impure.

Breakfast was served in the morning, as usual.

Eleven o'clock came, and the captain showed no signs of moving.

This apathy appeared incomprehensible to Mont.

Without any difficulty the vessel could have gone out to sea, risen in mid-ocean, and taken in fresh air.

"It is very odd we don't move," he remarked.

"I can't understand it," said the professor. "But everything is so remarkable on board this ship that I have ceased to wonder at anything."

"I've had a taste of niggers, and don't want another," said Stump, who was lying on a mattress with his leg bound up.

"Hark at the reptiles! What a thundering row they're kicking up!" remarked Mont.

"I never heard such a racket," answered Carl; "our skipper must be out of his head not to start the vipers."

The captain appeared in the doorway.

There was a pleasant smile on his face, and he did not seem at all alarmed at the menacing aspect of affairs.

Roy Rockwood

"Gentlemen," he said, "we resume our voyage at twelve o'clock exactly."

"It is now a quarter to," said the professor, regarding his chronometer.

"Precisely. I shall open the flap, and take in air directly."

"And the niggers?" said Mont.

"The Papouans?" replied the captain, shrugging his shoulders.

"Won't they get in?"

"How?"

"Easily enough, by walking down the ladder. They can do that when the flap is up, and can kill us all without any trouble."

"Gentlemen," said Captain Vindex, "the Papouans will not descend the staircase, although the flap is open."

They regarded this singular man in amazement.

"You do not understand me," he continued. "Come to the bottom of the ladder, and you shall see."

"Shall we take our guns?" asked the professor.

"Not the slightest necessity."

"At least your slaves are armed?"

"They are all at their work; follow me," said the captain.

They obeyed his order, and walked to the foot of the metal ladder.

The captain folded his arms, and stood by the side of the professor.

Mont and Carl were together.

Even Stump had crawled along the passage to see what would happen.

Captain Vindex made a sign to a slave, who, touching a spring, caused a trapdoor in the back of the *Searcher* to fly open.

The sunshine descended in a flood.

Terrible cries of rage and triumph were heard, and a swarm of natives appeared on all sides.

At least twenty made a rush at the ladder, brandishing their tomahawks and spears, while they uttered fierce yells and scraps of war songs.

The first who grasped the railing, and placed his foot on the ladder, gave a bound back, and the most fearful shrieks burst from his quivering lips. A second, a third, and a fourth did the same.

What invisible force was at work Mont did not know. He thought the days of magic and sorcery had returned.

A score of Papouans tried to descend; but they had no sooner made the attempt than they instantly retreated, yelling dismally, and threw themselves into the sea.

"Stunning," said Mont. "It's fine, but I don't know how you do it."

The captain smiled.

To get a better view, Mont put one foot on the staircase and one hand on the railing.

He immediately withdrew them, uttering a cry which was loud enough to wake the dead.

"Oh, oh!" he cried.

"What's up?" exclaimed Carl, who could not help laughing.

"I see the dodge now," said Mont; "it's an electric battery applied to the metal of the staircase, and whoever touches it has a shock. I've had it before at Coney Island, and at fairs. You pay a dime and get electrified."

"Ah!" ejaculated the professor, upon whom a light began to dawn.

"You are right," said the captain calmly. "I have connected the brass staircase with the powerful storage battery that gives us light and power, and the ignorant savages are frightened at they know not what. If they had persisted in their attempt to enter the ship I should have applied all my electrical force, and they would have fallen as dead as flies on a fly paper; but I did not wish to harm them. They are enemies unworthy of my hatred."

The news of the dreadful and mysterious pains which they felt were spread by the shocked natives to their friends.

Alarmed and horrified, they beat a precipitate retreat,

swimming and rowing back to the shore.

In half an hour the beach was deserted, and all flew away from the sea fiend whose nature they could not understand.

"They take us for the Old Nick," said Mont.

"Twelve o'clock," exclaimed the captain, who was always as punctual as fate; "I said we should sail at twelve."

At this moment the engines began to revolve, and the *Searcher* skimmed over the surface of the sea like a bird.

The air was soon taken into the reservoirs, the flap or panel was closed, and sinking into the bosom of the waves, she glided along, moved by her powerful screw, like a big fish; only the helmsman, sitting in his solitary place of lookout, being responsible for her management.

Roy Rockwood

CHAPTER XXIV

A PEARL WORTH A FORTUNE

They traversed the ocean at a depth of about a hundred yards from the surface.

The health of the captives continued good.

Stump was the only grumbler; the others read and talked, resigning themselves to their fate, and waiting the next adventure which should befall them in their singular voyage.

"I tell you what it is, sir," exclaimed Stump one day; "I wish I could get my fist near that there captain. If I wouldn't give him a knockout I'd let a whale come and eat me."

"What have you to grumble at, my friend?" inquired Professor Woddle. "You are comfortably housed, well fed, and have a constant source of excitement in the movements of this remarkable ship."

"Bother the ship. Why didn't she strike on a rock and bust up?" said Stump. "I'd rather be back to Nautical Hall any day than here."

"Bide your time, my lad," continued the professor;

"something will happen some day."

"Very prob'ble, sir, but it's waiting for it to turn up as I don't like. Just shove me alongside of that blessed captain, and if I don't give him—"

"Stump," interrupted Mont, "you shut up. I wouldn't mind being back to the Hall myself, but finding fault won't take us there."

"Certainly, sir. I don't have much chance of talking. I shall forget my own language soon; but no matter, I am only a hired boy, I know, and, of course, shouldn't have no feelings."

Mont took the trouble to pacify him, explaining that to provoke a quarrel with the captain would not in any way improve their position.

On the contrary, it might deprive them of the little liberty and comforts they now enjoyed, and make their miserable condition much worse.

Stump saw this and promised to be quiet.

He was a strong lad for his age, as hard as iron, and brave as a young lion.

"Just promise me this, sir," he said.

"What?"

"If I see a good chance of stepping it, you'll be with me?"

"Like a shot. But we mustn't do anything rash, you know, Stump," replied Mont. "Captain Vindex is not to be trifled with. A man who can build a ship like this, make electricity take the place of steam, and so store the air as to make it sufficient for use for twenty-four hours, is one of those great spirits who think of everything, and with whom we cannot hope to cope on equal terms."

"Don't know so much about that, sir," said Stump. "I once had a round with a professional boxer and laid him low in two minutes."

Mont laughed, and the conversation dropped.

The voyage continued to the Indian Sea, and was not remarkable for anything more exciting than the capture of several turtles in nets, and the shooting of various sea birds, which supplied an agreeable addition to the comforts of the table.

In the Indian Sea they encountered hundreds of the nautilus tribe floating gracefully on the surface of the water, their tiny sails spread, catching the wind, and looking like little ships.

One day Captain Vindex entered.

"Would you like to see the banks upon which grow the oysters which contain the pearls?" asked the captain.

"Under the sea?" said Mont.

"An excursion, submarine?" said the professor.

"Precisely so. Are you inclined to go?"

"Very much, indeed," replied all in chorus, with the exception of Stump.

"This is not the time of year for the pearl divers to be at work," said the captain, "though we may see one or two. I will bring the ship nearer land, and show you some of the treasures of the deep. They fish for pearls in the Gulf of Bengal, in the Indian seas, as well as those of China and Japan, off the coast of South America, and in the Gulf of Panama and that of California, but it is at Ceylon that they find the richest harvest."

"That is a fact," said the professor; "the richest pearls, as you say, are found here."

"Right," said the captain. "We, however, shall see more than any diver ever dreams of. Perhaps I shall find my pearl worth a million, for which I have searched so long. I shall be at your service, gentlemen, in a few hours."

When the captain had departed the professor was very grave.

Carl and Mont were delighted at the prospect of finding pearls, but Stump bit his nails in silence.

"I'll take home a pearl or two for luck!" exclaimed Mont.

"If you ever get home, sir," remarked Stump, half aloud.

"You'll go with us, won't you?" asked Mont.

"I'll go wherever you and Master Carl go, Master Mont," replied Stump, "because it's my duty to watch over you. But I aint going to have no sort of friendship with that captain, not by a jugful!"

"He's all right, when you know him."

"Is he? Then I don't want to know him."

Turning to the professor, Mont exclaimed:

"Shall we have good sport, sir?"

"Most likely," answered Mr. Woddle.

"Are there many sharks about?"

"It is no use disguising the fact. The sea hereabouts swarms with them. I should not like to meet one under the waves. A pearl has been called by poets a tear of the sea, and anything more lovely around a maiden's neck cannot be conceived. I have a strong wish to hunt for those tears of the sea, and behold them growing in their shells, but Heaven protect us from the sharks."

Stump disappeared for a brief space, and returned with a long harpoon.

"What have you got there?" asked Mont.

"It's a reg'lar pig-sticker, isn't it, sir?" remarked Stump, regarding it admiringly.

"It does look as if it could give an ugly prod," remarked Carl.

"They call it a harpoon; thing for sticking whales. Me and Number One, that's the nigger as waits on us, is friends, sir, and he's given me this to fight the darned sharkses with."

"Bravo, Stump!" exclaimed Carl.

"It would be 'Bravo Stump,' if I could rip up an inch or two of that captain, and seize the blessed ship!" rejoined the boy with a scowl.

Mont said nothing in reply, but waited patiently for the signal which would summon him and his companions to the captain's side.

It came an hour or two before daybreak.

A negro summoned them to the platform, near which the boat attached to the ship was riding.

It was manned by four men, and when all the party were on board the negroes began to row toward the island.

At six o'clock the day broke. They were a few miles from the land, which was distinctly visible, with a few trees scattered here and there.

The captain stood up in the boat, and narrowly regarded the sea. At last he gave a sign, and the anchor was lowered.

"Here we are," said the captain. "Put on your divers' caps, gentlemen, and follow me."

The heavy sea garments were quickly put on.

The electric lamps were not needed, because the depth was not great.

Besides, the electric light would attract the sharks, who were creatures they could not afford to despise.

The only arm given to each of the party was a long, sharp knife.

Captain Vindex set the example of springing into the sea, the others following him as soon as they were thoroughly equipped.

The negroes remained in the boat awaiting their return.

A depth of about three yards and a half did not give them a very great submersion.

To be supplied with condensed air, to be armed, and well lighted up by the sun was delightful. They walked along the bottom of the sea, easily seeing the smallest object on all sides of them.

After some little walking they came to several oyster banks, from which the shells containing the valuable pearls were dragged by the hands of the divers.

There were millions of them, and the mine seemed inexhaustible.

They could not stop to examine everything, for it was necessary to follow the captain everywhere.

The road was uneven; sometimes Mont could raise his arm and put his hand out of the water; at others, he was descending a slope, and the sun's rays were not so vivid.

Everything became more obscure, and great shells were seen sticking to curiously shaped rocks.

After a time a large grotto appeared before them, dimly lighted.

The captain entered, followed by the rest of the party, the professor eagerly taking note of everything.

Stump carried his harpoon, which was a good deal longer than himself; and the two boys eagerly looked for pearls, as if they expected to find them lying at their feet.

Descending an inclined plane, Captain Vindex stopped and pointed out an object which they had not hitherto perceived.

It was an oyster of gigantic size.

Lying alone upon the granite rock, it took up a large space, and never had the professor even heard of such a huge bivalve.

The shells were open a little, as if the oyster was feeding, which enabled the captain to introduce his knife.

Keeping the two shells open by both ends of his knife, he pushed back the flesh of the oyster and revealed a pearl as big as a small cocoanut.

It was a pearl worth at least a hundred thousand dollars.

CHAPTER XXV

THE MAN OF MYSTERY

Mont advanced to the oyster, and stretched out his hand as if he would have seized the pearl, but he was disappointed.

By a sudden movement the captain withdrew his knife, and the two shells came together with a sharp snap.

Satisfied with showing them this treasure of the deep, he turned round, and retraced his steps, leaving the precious pearl behind them.

Incomprehensible man, he was now more than ever a mystery to our hero.

He allowed them to seek and take numerous other pearls, but would not let them touch that he had shown them.

Again they wandered along the bottom of the sea, beholding many things worthy of observation.

Sometimes the bank was so shallow that their heads came above the water; at others they sank several yards below.

Suddenly the captain stopped, and by a movement of his

hand ordered the party to conceal themselves behind a projecting rock.

He pointed to the liquid mass in front of them, and all followed with their eyes the direction indicated.

About five yards off a shadow came between the party and the rays of the sun.

Mont thought of the "sea butcher," as the divers of Ceylon call the shark, and trembled a little at the idea.

But he deceived himself, for this time he had nothing to fear from the monster of the ocean.

A living man, an Indian, as black as ink, shot through the water, doubtless an early fisher for pearls.

The bottom of his canoe could be seen up above, a few feet beyond his head.

Arriving at the bottom, which was about five yards deep, he fell on his knees, let go the stone he had held between his feet to sink with more rapidity, and began to rake up the oysters from the bank with both hands.

A cord was around his waist, the other end being attached to his boat, and this he pulled at when he wanted to rise.

To his loins was attached a little bag, into which he put the oysters as fast as he could gather them.

The Indian did not see anyone, and if he had he would have been so alarmed at the strange spectacle of curious-looking beings walking at ease at the bottom of the sea that he would quickly have retired.

Several times he remounted and plunged again, not getting more than a dozen oysters at each dip.

It appeared as if he risked his life for very little return, as in a score of oysters he might not find a pearl worth having.

All at once, while on his knees, he made a gesture of terror, and seized his rope to ascend to the surface.

A gigantic mass appeared close to the wretched diver.

It was a huge shark, which advanced diagonally toward him, his terrible jaws open wide.

The Indian threw himself on one side and avoided the bite of the shark, but not the action of his tail.

Mont thought he heard the jaws snap, but he had not much time to think, as he saw the diver thrown down by a blow of the animal's tail and stretched upon the ground.

All this was done in a few seconds, and then the shark returned, lying upon his back, in order the better to bite and divide the Indian in halves.

Mont was about to rush forward to attempt to save the miserable wretch's life, when he was pushed rudely back by Captain Vindex.

In his hand he held a knife, and was evidently prepared to battle for his life against the shark.

The latter, just about to seize the Indian and snap him up, perceived his new adversary and, replacing himself upon his belly, directed himself rapidly toward him.

He waited coolly the attack of the shark, which was one of the largest of its species, and when it charged him, he stepped quickly aside and plunged his knife into its belly up to the hilt.

Then commenced a fearful combat.

The shark began to bleed dreadfully, tinging the sea in such a manner as to hide the two in a sea of blood.

As the water cleared a little, Mont saw the captain, caught by one of the creature's fins, stabbing at it as fast as he could, but not being able to give it a deathblow. The shark lashed the sea with fury, and almost prevented the professor and his friends from keeping their footing, though they were some distance off.

Neither the professor, Mont, nor Carl dared to go to the help of the captain, for it seemed as if the shark would bite them in two, and they lost their presence of mind for a time.

But Mont soon recovered, and then, catching Stump's harpoon, he darted forward to do his best.

With his teeth set, he precipitated himself toward the shark, and struck it a terrible blow in the flank.

Again the sea was saturated with blood.

The shark agitated the water with indescribable fury, for our hero had not missed his aim.

It was the death agony of the monster.

Stricken to the heart, he struggled gallantly, but was powerless for further evil.

As the immense creature was dying, Mont pulled the captain from under him, and at the same moment the Indian, coming to himself, detached the stone from his feet and shot upward.

Following the example of the pearl diver, the captain struck the ground with his heels, as did the others, and all were soon at the surface.

The Indian had regained his canoe, but he was lying at the bottom in a half-fainting condition.

Satisfying himself that the poor fellow would live, and was not seriously injured, the captain signaled to his companions to descend, leaving the Indian gazing at them with haggard eyes, thinking he had seen some supernatural beings.

Walking as fast as they could along the bottom of the sea, they came in time to the anchor of their boat, reascended to the surface, and, taking their seats, removed their head-cases with a feeling of relief.

The negroes immediately began to row back to the *Searcher*.

Captain Vindex was the first to speak.

"Thank you, my lad," he said, extending his hand to Mont.

"It's nothing," rejoined our hero bluntly; "you saved my life when we were wrecked, and I have now saved yours with my harpoon. We are equal now, and I owe you nothing."

A sickly smile sat on the captain's lips for a second, and that was all.

"Lay to it!" he cried to his men. "Pull to the *Searcher*."

At half-past eight in the morning they were again on board of the ship, having been absent a little more than three hours.

To Mont the captain was more difficult to understand than ever.

He had risked his own life to save that of a poor Indian whom he had never seen before, and was never likely to see again.

This showed that he could not have a bad heart.

His heart was not entirely dead, whatever his faults might be.

As if the captain guessed Mont's thoughts, he observed to him at the bottom of the staircase on board the ship:

"That Indian belonged to an oppressed race. I also am one of the oppressed, and to my last breath I shall continue to be so. You recognize now the bond of union between us?"

CHAPTER XXVI

THROUGH THE EARTH

The ship again continued her way, traveling toward the Persian Gulf.

If Captain Vindex wanted to visit Europe, it was clear that he would have to go around the Cape of Good Hope, but that did not appear to be his design.

He went direct to the Red Sea, and, as the Isthmus of Suez was not then pierced by a canal, there was no outlet to the Mediterranean.

This puzzled the professor very much.

One morning the captain sought his prisoners, and said to the professor:

"To-morrow we shall be in the Mediterranean."

Mr. Woddle looked at him with astonishment.

"Does that surprise you?" he continued, with a smile.

"Certainly it does, though I thought I had given up being

astonished since I have been on board your ship."

"You are a man of science; why should you be astonished?"

"Because you must travel with the speed of lightning almost to East Africa and round the Cape of Good Hope."

"I did not say I was going to do so," replied the captain.

"You can't go overland, since there is no canal through the Isthmus of Suez—"

"But one can go under land," interrupted the captain.

"Under land," answered the professor, holding up his hand.

"Undoubtedly," said Captain Vindex calmly. "For a long while nature has made underneath this tongue of land what men are trying to do now on the surface."

"Does there exist a passage?"

"Yes, a passage or tunnel, which at fifty feet depth touches a solid rock."

"How did you discover it—by chance?"

"No," said the captain. "I guessed that such a tunnel existed, and I have been through it several times."

"Well," said the professor, "we live to learn. Our fathers never dreamed of gas, of railways, of telegraphs, and I did not suspect the existence of your wonderful ship."

"Shortly, my dear sir," said the captain, "your children—that is to say, the next generation—will travel through the air in flying machines; your railway engines will own electricity as their motive power. There is no end to scientific discovery; the world is in its infancy. We are just emerging from barbarism. Wait and watch, that's my motto. You must not be surprised at anything in these days."

"You are right—we are on the march," said the professor.

The day passed, and at half-past nine the *Searcher* rose to the surface to receive her supply of air.

Nothing disturbed the silence but the cry of the pelican and other birds of the night, with the occasional sound of the escaping steam of a steamer traveling toward the Far East.

Mont could not rest below, and at once ascended to the platform to breath the fresh air. In the darkness he saw a pale light, discolored by the fog, which burned about a mile off.

"A lighthouse," he said.

The captain was by his side, and quietly replied:

"It is the floating lightship of Suez."

"We are near the mouth of the tunnel, I suppose? Is the entrance easy?"

"No," said Captain Vindex, "it is difficult. I always steer the ship myself, and if you like to come into the wheelhouse with me I will show you the way. In a moment the *Searcher* will sink, and we shall not rise till we are in the Mediterranean."

Mont followed the captain into the pilot's cabin, which was at the bow of the vessel, the wheel working the rudder by long chains carried aft.

The cabin measured six feet square, four round windows of thick plate-glass enabled the helmsman to see on all sides, and the electric light, thrown well forward, made everything as clear as day.

A strong negro, with an eye like a hawk, was at the wheel, but he gave the spokes to the captain and fell back.

"Now," exclaimed the Wizard of the Sea, "let us search for our passage."

Electric wires communicated with the engine room, so it was easy to communicate directly with the engineers by pressing a knob of metal.

Touching this knob, the speed of the screw lessened considerably.

For about an hour the ship passed by a bank of sand, which was varied by rocks, on which Mont saw all kinds of sea weeds, coral formations, and curious fish agitating their fins in alarm at the apparition of the *Searcher*.

At half-past ten a long and large gallery appeared in front, black and apparently deep.

The ship entered this gloomy tunnel boldly, and an unaccustomed rushing sound made itself heard against the sides, which arose from the waters of the Red Sea rushing into the Mediterranean.

Following the current with the speed of an arrow, the ship made its way, though the engines were reversed and the screw went backward to abate the velocity of its progress.

A single false turn of the wheel, and the *Searcher* would

have been dashed to atoms against the ironlike rocks on each side, above, and below.

Mont held his breath.

He could see nothing but the foaming waters, made transparent by the electric light.

Half an hour later the captain gave up the helm to the negro, and, turning to our hero, exclaimed:

"We are in the Mediterranean."

In less than half an hour the ship, carried by the current, had traversed the Isthmus of Suez.

The next morning they came to the surface, and were able to breathe the fresh air again.

Stump was in high spirits when he found that they were near civilization again, because he thought they had a chance of escaping, and this idea was always uppermost in his mind.

He spoke to his companions about it, and they all agreed to follow him if a good opportunity offered.

CHAPTER XXVII

THE ESCAPE—CONCLUSION

The ship traveled leisurely along the Mediterranean, often rising in sight of land and lying like a log upon the water.

In the evening it was the custom of the prisoners to play at checkers, dominoes, or some game they liked; and after the fourth day in the Mediterranean, Stump, instead of putting the games on the table, shut the door, and, in a mysterious way, exclaimed:

"I've squared the nigger!"

"Which?" asked Mont.

"Number One. He as waits upon us. His real name's Smunko. I've found that out. Me and he's firm friends. I've told him I want to bolt, and he says he shan't let on to the skipper, or any of them, though they are all a lot of spies."

"Perhaps he's one, too," observed the professor, smiling.

"Not he, sir," answered the boy; "Smunko's right enough. He's going to keep all the other chaps quiet, some dark night, when we are near the land. Then we are to go on the platform and swim for our lives."

"A very good arrangement, if it can be carried out," remarked the professor. "But I fear your friend Smunko is not to be depended upon."

Stump was indignant.

"The fact is," went on the professor, "I don't want to discourage the lad, but I have no wish that he should do anything rash, and involve us in a mess. The captain might doom us to solitary confinement. At present we are treated liberally, if we are prisoners."

"All right, sir," replied Stump, "I'll turn it up as far as you are concerned. If Master Mont likes to come with me, all well and good; if not he can let it alone. I know my game, and I mean to stick to it."

"Don't show your nasty temper, Stump," said our hero.

"Aint being cooped up here like a turkey in a pen, fatting for Christmas, enough to rile a bishop?" asked the boy. "But I shan't say no more. When all's ready I'll give you one more chance, and if you aint with me, I'm off alone."

It was impossible to check Stump's will. The only one who had any influence over him was Mont.

He was a boy rudely brought up, unaccustomed to control his passions, and having a decided character, but to our hero he was deeply attached.

The next day the ship floated near an island, which the professor declared to be the Isle of Cyprus.

In the evening Stump whispered to Mont:

"Now, sir, all's ready. Smunko's piping off the other blacks; we're not a quarter of a mile from the land."

Mont's heart beat high.

"Tell the others," he said.

"No; let you and I go together."

"I can't leave Carl, and the professor is one of us."

In this Mont was firm.

He would not leave the *Searcher* without Carl and the professor.

So the two were told that all was ready.

"Come on, now," said Mont. "We must not lose our chance."

With the valuable pearls they had secured in the Indian Ocean in their pockets, the others followed Mont to the deck.

All hearts beat loudly.

"There is a boat!" whispered Carl. "Come on."

He dropped into the sea, and the others did the same.

Not far away floated a log, and to this they clung.

They paddled with their hands, and were soon some distance away from the submarine monster.

Then they cried for help.

The boat they had seen came in their direction.

They were seen, and the natives from the island let out a shout.

Then suddenly Captain Vindex appeared on the deck of the *Searcher*.

He shook his fist at the party.

Stump laughed at him; the others waved him off.

"She is going down!" cried Mont. "Quick, pull for the shore, before you are wrecked!"

The natives did not like the looks of the strange submarine ship, and they pulled with all strength.

By the agitation in the water the party knew the *Searcher* was after them.

But the shore was gained, and they were safe.

Then came a fearful shock.

In his eagerness to catch them Captain Vindex had allowed the *Searcher* to run into the rocks.

The submarine craft shot out of the water, and then—

Bang! Boom! Crash!

It was as if heaven and earth were splitting in twain.

The whole island shook, and all in the boat fell flat.

The *Searcher* had been blown to atoms.

The air was filled with flying bits of iron and steel.

Of course all on board were instantly killed.

It was a long while before Mont and his companions recovered.

"Out of it at last, thank Heaven!" murmured Professor Woddle, and all said "Amen."

A month later the little party returned to the United States.

Mont's widowed mother was overjoyed to see him alive, and Carl's parents were equally elated, and so were the many friends at Nautical Hall.

The pearls were equally divided, and to-day all of the party are rich men.

"But I wouldn't take another such trip," says Mont. "No, not to pick up all the hidden treasures of the ocean. After this I'm going to remain at Nautical Hall and take the balance of my sea training on land. I've had all I want of such submarine ships as the *Searcher*, and such mysterious men as was the Wizard of the Sea."

*   *   *   *   *

Choose from Thousands of 1stWorldLibrary Classics By

A. M. Barnard	Booth Tarkington	Edward Everett Hale
Ada Leverson	Boyd Cable	Edward J. O'Biren
Adolphus William Ward	Bram Stoker	Edward S. Ellis
Aesop	C. Collodi	Edwin L. Arnold
Agatha Christie	C. E. Orr	Eleanor Atkins
Alexander Aaronsohn	C. M. Ingleby	Eleanor Hallowell Abbott
Alexander Kielland	Carolyn Wells	Eliot Gregory
Alexandre Dumas	Catherine Parr Traill	Elizabeth Gaskell
Alfred Gatty	Charles A. Eastman	Elizabeth McCracken
Alfred Ollivant	Charles Amory Beach	Elizabeth Von Arnim
Alice Duer Miller	Charles Dickens	Ellem Key
Alice Turner Curtis	Charles Dudley Warner	Emerson Hough
Alice Dunbar	Charles Farrar Browne	Emilie F. Carlen
Allen Chapman	Charles Ives	Emily Bronte
Alleyne Ireland	Charles Kingsley	Emily Dickinson
Ambrose Bierce	Charles Klein	Enid Bagnold
Amelia E. Barr	Charles Hanson Towne	Enilor Macartney Lane
Amory H. Bradford	Charles Lathrop Pack	Erasmus W. Jones
Andrew Lang	Charles Romyn Dake	Ernie Howard Pie
Andrew McFarland Davis	Charles Whibley	Ethel May Dell
Andy Adams	Charles Willing Beale	Ethel Turner
Angela Brazil	Charlotte M. Braeme	Ethel Watts Mumford
Anna Alice Chapin	Charlotte M. Yonge	Eugene Sue
Anna Sewell	Charlotte Perkins Stetson	Eugenie Foa
Annie Besant	Clair W. Hayes	Eugene Wood
Annie Hamilton Donnell	Clarence Day Jr.	Eustace Hale Ball
Annie Payson Call	Clarence E. Mulford	Evelyn Everett-green
Annie Roe Carr	Clemence Housman	Everard Cotes
Annonaymous	Confucius	F. H. Cheley
Anton Chekhov	Coningsby Dawson	F. J. Cross
Archibald Lee Fletcher	Cornelis DeWitt Wilcox	F. Marion Crawford
Arnold Bennett	Cyril Burleigh	Fannie E. Newberry
Arthur C. Benson	D. H. Lawrence	Federick Austin Ogg
Arthur Conan Doyle	Daniel Defoe	Ferdinand Ossendowski
Arthur M. Winfield	David Garnett	Fergus Hume
Arthur Ransome	Dinah Craik	Florence A. Kilpatrick
Arthur Schnitzler	Don Carlos Janes	Fremont B. Deering
Arthur Train	Donald Keyhoe	Francis Bacon
Atticus	Dorothy Kilner	Francis Darwin
B.H. Baden-Powell	Dougan Clark	Frances Hodgson Burnett
B. M. Bower	Douglas Fairbanks	Frances Parkinson Keyes
B. C. Chatterjee	E. Nesbit	Frank Gee Patchin
Baroness Emmuska Orczy	E. P. Roe	Frank Harris
Baroness Orczy	E. Phillips Oppenheim	Frank Jewett Mather
Basil King	E. S. Brooks	Frank L. Packard
Bayard Taylor	Earl Barnes	Frank V. Webster
Ben Macomber	Edgar Rice Burroughs	Frederic Stewart Isham
Bertha Muzzy Bower	Edith Van Dyne	Frederick Trevor Hill
Bjornstjerne Bjornson	Edith Wharton	Frederick Winslow Taylor

Friedrich Kerst	Hayden Carruth	James Branch Cabell
Friedrich Nietzsche	Helent Hunt Jackson	James DeMille
Fyodor Dostoyevsky	Helen Nicolay	James Joyce
G.A. Henty	Hendrik Conscience	James Lane Allen
G.K. Chesterton	Hendy David Thoreau	James Lane Allen
Gabrielle E. Jackson	Henri Barbusse	James Oliver Curwood
Garrett P. Serviss	Henrik Ibsen	James Oppenheim
Gaston Leroux	Henry Adams	James Otis
George A. Warren	Henry Ford	James R. Driscoll
George Ade	Henry Frost	Jane Abbott
Geroge Bernard Shaw	Henry James	Jane Austen
George Cary Eggleston	Henry Jones Ford	Jane L. Stewart
George Durston	Henry Seton Merriman	Janet Aldridge
George Ebers	Henry W Longfellow	Jens Peter Jacobsen
George Eliot	Herbert A. Giles	Jerome K. Jerome
George Gissing	Herbert Carter	Jessie Graham Flower
George MacDonald	Herbert N. Casson	John Buchan
George Meredith	Herman Hesse	John Burroughs
George Orwell	Hildegard G. Frey	John Cournos
George Sylvester Viereck	Homer	John F. Kennedy
George Tucker	Honore De Balzac	John Gay
George W. Cable	Horace B. Day	John Glasworthy
George Wharton James	Horace Walpole	John Habberton
Gertrude Atherton	Horatio Alger Jr.	John Joy Bell
Gordon Casserly	Howard Pyle	John Kendrick Bangs
Grace E. King	Howard R. Garis	John Milton
Grace Gallatin	Hugh Lofting	John Philip Sousa
Grace Greenwood	Hugh Walpole	John Taintor Foote
Grant Allen	Humphry Ward	Jonas Lauritz Idemil Lie
Guillermo A. Sherwell	Ian Maclaren	Jonathan Swift
Gulielma Zollinger	Inez Haynes Gillmore	Joseph A. Altsheler
Gustav Flaubert	Irving Bacheller	Joseph Carey
H. A. Cody	Isabel Cecilia Williams	Joseph Conrad
H. B. Irving	Isabel Hornibrook	Joseph E. Badger Jr
H.C. Bailey	Israel Abrahams	Joseph Hergesheimer
H. G. Wells	Ivan Turgenev	Joseph Jacobs
H. H. Munro	J.G.Austin	Jules Vernes
H. Irving Hancock	J. Henri Fabre	Julian Hawthrone
H. R. Naylor	J. M. Barrie	Julie A Lippmann
H. Rider Haggard	J. M. Walsh	Justin Huntly McCarthy
H. W. C. Davis	J. Macdonald Oxley	Kakuzo Okakura
Haldeman Julius	J. R. Miller	Karle Wilson Baker
Hall Caine	J. S. Fletcher	Kate Chopin
Hamilton Wright Mabie	J. S. Knowles	Kenneth Grahame
Hans Christian Andersen	J. Storer Clouston	Kenneth McGaffey
Harold Avery	J. W. Duffield	Kate Langley Bosher
Harold McGrath	Jack London	Kate Langley Bosher
Harriet Beecher Stowe	Jacob Abbott	Katherine Cecil Thurston
Harry Castlemon	James Allen	Katherine Stokes
Harry Coghill	James Andrews	L. A. Abbot
Harry Houidini	James Baldwin	L. T. Meade

L. Frank Baum
Latta Griswold
Laura Dent Crane
Laura Lee Hope
Laurence Housman
Lawrence Beasley
Leo Tolstoy
Leonid Andreyev
Lewis Carroll
Lewis Sperry Chafer
Lilian Bell
Lloyd Osbourne
Louis Hughes
Louis Joseph Vance
Louis Tracy
Louisa May Alcott
Lucy Fitch Perkins
Lucy Maud Montgomery
Luther Benson
Lydia Miller Middleton
Lyndon Orr
M. Corvus
M. H. Adams
Margaret E. Sangster
Margret Howth
Margaret Vandercook
Margaret W. Hungerford
Margret Penrose
Maria Edgeworth
Maria Thompson Daviess
Mariano Azuela
Marion Polk Angellotti
Mark Overton
Mark Twain
Mary Austin
Mary Catherine Crowley
Mary Cole
Mary Hastings Bradley
Mary Roberts Rinehart
Mary Rowlandson
M. Wollstonecraft Shelley
Maud Lindsay
Max Beerbohm
Myra Kelly
Nathaniel Hawthrone
Nicolo Machiavelli
O. F. Walton
Oscar Wilde
Owen Johnson
P.G. Wodehouse
Paul and Mabel Thorne

Paul G. Tomlinson
Paul Severing
Percy Brebner
Percy Keese Fitzhugh
Peter B. Kyne
Plato
Quincy Allen
R. Derby Holmes
R. L. Stevenson
R. S. Ball
Rabindranath Tagore
Rahul Alvares
Ralph Bonehill
Ralph Henry Barbour
Ralph Victor
Ralph Waldo Emmerson
Rene Descartes
Ray Cummings
Rex Beach
Rex E. Beach
Richard Harding Davis
Richard Jefferies
Richard Le Gallienne
Robert Barr
Robert Frost
Robert Gordon Anderson
Robert L. Drake
Robert Lansing
Robert Lynd
Robert Michael Ballantyne
Robert W. Chambers
Rosa Nouchette Carey
Rudyard Kipling
Saint Augustine
Samuel B. Allison
Samuel Hopkins Adams
Sarah Bernhardt
Sarah C. Hallowell
Selma Lagerlof
Sherwood Anderson
Sigmund Freud
Standish O'Grady
Stanley Weyman
Stella Benson
Stella M. Francis
Stephen Crane
Stewart Edward White
Stijn Streuvels
Swami Abhedananda
Swami Parmananda
T. S. Ackland

T. S. Arthur
The Princess Der Ling
Thomas A. Janvier
Thomas A Kempis
Thomas Anderton
Thomas Bailey Aldrich
Thomas Bulfinch
Thomas De Quincey
Thomas Dixon
Thomas H. Huxley
Thomas Hardy
Thomas More
Thornton W. Burgess
U. S. Grant
Upton Sinclair
Valentine Williams
Various Authors
Vaughan Kester
Victor Appleton
Victor G. Durham
Victoria Cross
Virginia Woolf
Wadsworth Camp
Walter Camp
Walter Scott
Washington Irving
Wilbur Lawton
Wilkie Collins
Willa Cather
Willard F. Baker
William Dean Howells
William le Queux
W. Makepeace Thackeray
William W. Walter
William Shakespeare
Winston Churchill
Yei Theodora Ozaki
Yogi Ramacharaka
Young E. Allison
Zane Grey